Copyright

Are You Ready for the Yes?

How to Prep Your Personal Brand for Lucrative Opportunities

By

Audria Richmond

Founder and CEO of Building BIG Brands Agency

Ordering Information:

Special discounts are available on quantity purchases by corporations, associations, and others. For details, contact the publisher at the email address above.

Orders by U.S. trade bookstores and wholesalers. Please contact Building BIG Brands Publishing:

Tel: (901) 238-6859; or visit www.audriarichmond.com

(Paperback)

ISBN 13: 978-0-9980722-0-3

ISBN 10: 0-9980722-0-6

(E-Book)

ISBN 13: 978-0-9980722-1-0

ISBN 10: 0-9980722-1-4

Developmental Editing by: Stefanie Manns

Book Cover Design by: Audria Richmond

Interior Book Design by: Audria Richmond

Photography by: Stanley Parrish Jr.

Acknowledgments

It has been a long time coming. I am beyond grateful and thankful to be able to say thank you! I have such a big tribe of family, friends, and supporters (you know who you are) that I really love with all of my heart. I can't even believe that you are reading my very first book!

This feels beyond real. I have a lot of amazing people who have been in my corner since Day One, all the way back in 2008. Memphis, Tennessee will always be home for me and I am proud to be the daughter of Anthony Arnold Sr. and Shirley Ann Arnold. I love you, Momma and Daddy! Big thanks to all of my brothers and my sister Joanne Hartsfield for raising me when Momma had to work.

Thanks so much Calvin, my loving husband, for really having my back through it all. You have witnessed more than most people can imagine. You are my rock and I will forever be grateful for your presence. This book would not even be possible without my book-writing team! Big thanks to Stefanie Manns and Apryl Beverly. You ladies know how to throw down on some keys!

I could go on and on with all of the praise, but you have a **YES!** to claim! Let's get you prepared.

Activate Your Yes!

Before you dive into this book, I want you to know that you are at the beginning of an amazing journey. I have prepared a free toolkit just for this book. It includes worksheets, check-lists, case studies, book recommendations, and video training to enhance your experience.

Building your personal brand is a long process and should be treated as legacy building. I really don't want you to just glaze over the content discussed in this book. It's time for you to **ACTIVATE** your **YES!**

Claim your Toolkit at **www.readyfortheyes.com**. Don't forget to use the hashtags **#readyfortheyes** and **#areyourea-dyfortheyes** on social media so I can track and keep up with your efforts. I want to see you out there doing your thing!

Table of Contents

TABLE OF CONTENTS

PREFACE

Since we're homies (also known as friends, buddies, and Business BFFs) I have a confession.

Cue the Usher.

When I launched my personal brand in 2014, I was so scared to be front and center. It wasn't so much about people seeing my company, but about seeing Audria. I was so used to being behind the scenes that having the world's eyeballs on me terrified me.

Sure, I'd run a really successful photography studio in Memphis, Tennessee and created a thriving platform for up-and-coming local artists. My work became a passionate movement that grew beyond anything I thought possible, shifting the social and arts scene with tons of sold-out events and, in the midst of it all, I even published my own digital magazine which garnered spotlight and awards for my photography. No, I wasn't new to the marketing or graphic design game by a long shot. I knew my shit and I'd built a name and an exceptional professional reputation for myself and my companies. So when I decided it was time to branch out, I had a shitload of experience so I knew I was capable. But even with knowing that, I wasn't confident yet. My confidence was still on the come-up. At a little over twenty-eight years young, I'd been an entrepreneur for years. Yet this whole online marketing space was brand new for me.

But I didn't look like it.

Digital brick by brick, I built my personal brand from the ground up. I'd relentlessly studied how the major players in the market did it, and I coupled what I learned with what I already knew in order to come out swinging. I leveraged my photography know-how and started with a professional photo shoot. I designed a killer website and graphics so people could easily find me, learn more about my work, and interact with me. I set up a customer relationship management system and created contracts so that when I closed a client, I had an onboarding workflow prepared and in place. As my visibility increased and I began to generate more buzz on social media, I got to know people by showing up at industry events, both online and offline. I established relationships. I launched a poppin' podcast, a YouTube channel for videos, and started writing my blog on digital platforms like *Medium*.

Everything about my personal brand screamed, "Hey, Everybody! I'm Audria and I am about this business life!" No shortcuts. No sidesteps. No stuttering when it came to my work or my worth.

Within six months, I'd crushed my monthly revenue goal and by the end of my first year, I'd made my first six figures. I had bloggers and publishers checking for me and knocking down my inbox for interviews. I was reaping opportunities that people who had been in the business for ten years or more weren't.

I was kicking ass and taking names.

Me. The chick who was literally a virtual nobody less than a year before.

All because I came out of the gate like a pro—from Day One.

Aside from an abundance of blessings, my success is attributed to a willingness to do the work it took to get people to know and respect my name. I knew I couldn't simply show up on the scene with a weak whisper and command the premium pricing that I knew my work warranted. I knew I had to show up in a certain way—with certain attributes in place—so that I'd be taken seriously, not only by my ideal clients but by my peers too. If I encountered an exciting opportunity that aligned with my brand or a client who I felt good about working with, I could jump on it without thinking twice.

I was ready for the yes.

I share my story, a few years and hundreds of clients later because I want you to know that I am not some superstar who just fell into big business. I didn't just write my own fairy tale (also known as the business plan) and stare at it. I didn't just fantasize about getting it. I didn't just study without taking steps or quietly set up a little Facebook fan page and pray that somebody I knew would see it and tell somebody else.

I had a plan. I had an idea and an expertise that I believed in. I worked really hard. I had guts.

And guess what? I have so much left over that I have some to share.

Need some?

Keep reading.

TELL ME YOUR DREAM AND I'LL TELL YOU WHY

YOU DON'T HAVE IT—YET

Whenever I sit down with a potential client, I start with an in-depth personal brand audit to assess where the person is, and more importantly, where they want to go. I always allow the client to go first, inviting them to take a really good, hard look at their existing brand and rate it honestly. My questionnaire walks them through their personal brands from tha roota to tha toota, from logo to last published blog post. We get in there so I know everything there is to know about them and the businesses they've built—or not built—so far.

But before we dig into the results, I love to ask the question, "So tell me, what would you like to be known for?"

With stars in their eyes, they begin to tell me who they want to be when they grow up. They share how they want to see their faces on the covers of best-selling books and sit on couches of talk shows on major networks. Their heart's desire is to host sold-out conferences with hundreds of people. They rattle off the names of their idols in the personal development or media industry (people I am sure you know and love too). And before I can get a word in edgewise, the conversation swiftly turns to a list of reasons why they'll never reach so-and-so's level.

I am not that good of a public speaker.

I don't have thousands of Facebook or Instagram followers.

I feel like I need to invest in a few more coaching programs before I can really jump out there.

I don't have enough publicity yet.

After having so many of these conversations, I started to read between the lines and, just like that, it began to dawn on me what was *really* going on. Everyone I talked to had the basics. They had a desire to be entrepreneurs, a passion for their businesses, and really wanted to help people. But they had not researched the market enough to have some idea about what to do to get a business off the ground. Many of them weren't rocking in their industries to a certain degree, booking clients, or making any money so they saw themselves as inferior to the business leaders that they aspired to be.

Why?

Because they had somehow convinced themselves that success came easy. They'd drunk the Bey-ade and were convinced that super successful people just woke up like that.

Nothing could be further from the truth.

I wish I could tell you these people had some sort of magic, but they don't.

Now, don't get me wrong, they're brilliant, they're constantly innovating ahead of the curve, and each and every one of them likely works their asses off. But that is not the complete formula or the only reason why they are iconic.

The difference between them and you is not billions of dollars, a high-dollar PR firm, or a captive audience of millions of people. It's not their stunning good looks or bright, white teeth. And it's not their star power, celebrity friends, or global influence, either.

It's their willingness to be front and center. Visible. Recognized. Known.

Their dreams have become their realities because **they aren't afraid to be seen**.

The hyper-successful influencers and moguls that you see everywhere today aren't afraid to allow people to see them because they recognize that in order for the world to connect, to want to hear what they have to say and buy what they need to sell, they have to come from behind their businesses and actually get in front of people every day.

So they speak on stages. They put their words and thoughts into books that you snatch off of the shelves. They sit down with journalists to share their personal stories and ideas on television, radio, and in print. They build relationships with you by telling you what they think and positioning themselves, in your mind, as experts and people who know what in the hell they're talking about. You buy their smartphones and tablets, attend their events, and watch their networks because they do something for you. You connect with them. And you say "Hell, yes!" to them because you believe in them and what they have to say.

As a consumer, you don't want to entrust your money to someone who doesn't have a clue or who you sense doesn't quite have their stuff together. You want a real person, a real relationship, a real expert.

The key to joining the ranks of the tycoons on your vision board (or better yet, your Yes! Board) is to develop a powerful, profitable personal brand. When your brand is on fire and running on all cylinders, it means the world can Google you and discover your website. That website is so well designed, engaging, and informative that a potential client or that billionaire business owner who wants to offer you the shot of a lifetime is interested enough to continue learning more about you. So they take a peek at your social media pages and find current and compelling content there. They can hop over to Periscope or YouTube and find you, all smiles, in front of a camera teaching your behind off on your topic of expertise. Your blog posts and your latest book are both getting rave reviews from readers. You're saying all the right things in all the right places.

It's clear that you know your stuff.

And that's what gets you in the major leagues. But it all starts with letting people know that you're human. And a human with a lot to say about the work you love to do.

That's the difference between you—and them. The people who you know and love in the world feel they've put in the work and somebody needs to hear about it. More than ego, becoming the face of your business is the responsibility of any expert, entrepreneur, or CEO. Anyone who has worked hard to build something, scratched and saved to make a dream come true, and is willing to fight to make a space for themselves in this world deserves to be seen.

And so do you, Love.

IT ALL STARTS WITH YOUR NAME

Before we go any further, let me tell you something.

I see you.

I know you've been slinking around in the shadows of the market because you don't think you have what it takes.

I know that even though you are amazing at what you do,

you're afraid somebody may yank the covers off of your head and call you a fraud.

I know you are playing peek-a-boo with your business—and with your profits.

All of that BS stops right now. *Today.*

You wouldn't have spent the last three years or more giving away services for free—repeatedly and on-demand—if you weren't great at something. You wouldn't have invested the time to research DIY websites and bought tickets to all of those conferences so you could learn from the best of the best.

Hell, you wouldn't have picked up this book or read this far if you didn't at least have an idea that you have something that somebody in this world wants and needs.

I am here to tell you what you already know. When God created you, He created something beautiful. He gave you an incredible, unique asset that can be packaged and delivered to change somebody's life and to make money.

What you know means something. What you do means something. Your name *means something*.

When you understand the power of your name, you will make millions.

A powerful and profitable personal brand is built on the

foundation of one thing—your name. When your name becomes recognizable and synonymous with quality, expertise, and credibility, the world is yours. Not only does your name enable you to reap today, but it gives you the agility to create businesses and opportunities that will last a lifetime. Your name becomes your brand. And your brand becomes your legacy.

The world would not have expected *The Oprah Winfrey Show* to grow and evolve, but was perfectly okay (to the tune of billions of dollars) for Oprah Winfrey, the woman behind the show, to act, build a media empire, launch her own network, go out on a multi-city national speaking tour, and endorse products and people she believes in. If Tyler Perry had just hidden behind Madea's skirt on the stage and never let his audiences and the world see him, it wouldn't have been possible for him to successfully set up his own studio, produce box office hit after hit, or join forces with the OWN Network to bring his characters to the small screen. Fans follow Oprah, Tyler, the CEO of Apple—take your pick—because of the strength of their personal brands.

They come for the person first, then the product.

An established personal brand grants you the agility to move and grow along with your business and interests. While motivational speaking to high school students may be ideal for you now, your message won't have the same impact when you're eighty years old standing in front of a group of kids. But if you've built a personal brand as an empowerment speaker for people in transition, you can tailor your message, content, and products to capture a new audience.

You can outgrow a company, but you can't outgrow your expertise. And you surely can't outgrow yourself.

You've got one identity. One brain. One fingerprint. One name. And nobody can take that away from you.

IF THIS SOUNDS LIKE YOU, KEEP READING BECAUSE
I WROTE THIS BOOK FOR YOU

If you picked up this book, chances are you've had an opportunity to grow, to take your business to the next level, and you missed the shot. The good news is the ball will probably get passed to you again, and this time, you need to be ready.

This book is for you.

I wrote this book for the entrepreneur who knows they have more work to do and, more importantly, they're willing to do it. In my years of working with clients and taking brands from pitiful to profitable, I've met a few folks who have some things in common.

Does one of them sound like you?

- **The Faceless CEO.** You started a company so you could make it to the top. Congratulations, you did it. But now you're there—alone. Because you're hiding behind your logo, your business has no face. The world has never heard your voice, your story, your passion, your personality. People want to know who you are, but you're holding up the wall at the school dance, terrified that someone will ask you to hit the floor (even though you're secretly wishing somebody would grab you by the hand so you can sweat out those curls and shake what yo' momma gave you). There's a mic waiting with your name on it.

- **The Company Without Clients. (Ouch).** You put it all on the line and went into business for yourself. You dotted your Is and crossed your Ts. The LLC is set up. The Vistaprint order is in. But you found that actually getting clients in the door was a lot harder than it looks. You may not be hiding completely, but you're showing up without the 4 Cs: consistency, credibility, connection, and cohesiveness. You're spinning your wheels and spending a lot of money in the process trying to get something, anything, going. You need more people and more profits—now.

- **The Kick-A** Expert Who Nobody Knows.** Also known as the side hustler. Can you sew a couture gown without a pattern? Change oil and replace an engine with your eyes closed? Are you the community's go-to cook or a genius in all things holistic health? Chances are you have a massive amount of knowledge about something and a skill set that a lot of people would love to pay you for, even if you have a 9-5 that you intend to keep. But they have no idea that you even exist.

- **The Business Owner With No Brand.** A few people have gathered from your Facebook page that you have some sort of business, but the interest—and the buck—has stopped there. If you weren't posting a cute quote every once in a while, who would know you were alive, much less had a company?

WHAT YOU DO IS WHAT YOU GET

This book is divided into seven phases, each representing a must-have element of a powerful, profitable personal brand. The framework is based on one of my top-selling, signature programs that my clients invest thousands of dollars in. The information that you'll find in these pages is based on years on top of years of research that I've done on personal branding and marketing, client case studies, and the genius that God granted me to, quite frankly, be the best at what I do. (Hey, when you got it, own it!)

If you read this book and apply what you learn, you're going to get your money's worth—and then some. The tools, techniques, and resources throughout this book will make you known, make you respected, and make you money.

Here's my big promise to you:

If you do just one thing in each of these phases, you will have a profitable, personal brand.

Do them all, and I'll see your face on billboards and hear your name shouted out from the stage at the next Kanye concert. (Okay, that may or may not happen. But if that's your dream, I can help you get there.)

Now here's my big challenge for you:

Dig deep and be willing to do what it seriously takes to be great.

This book is designed to teach you the fundamentals of any personal brand and to position you to rival any competitor out there in the market. By the end of it, you will have the know-how to create the brand and the business that moves you out of the shadows and into the spotlight—where you belong.

Remember those guts I loaned you? Grab 'em and let's get it!

Part One

MINDSET PREPARATION

CHAPTER ONE
WHAT DOES IT MEAN TO BE READY FOR THE YES?

"So if you stay ready, you ain't gotta get ready, and that's how I run my life."

Those are words from mega actor and media mogul, Will Smith. His career accomplishments, both in front of and behind the camera, go without saying, and while some could argue that a superstar of this caliber could just rest on his laurels and chill, it's clear he has no intention of doing anything close. Instead, he is constantly in preparation mode. Be it bodybuilding like a beast or studying his craft with the tenacity of an extra on set, when—not if—Will gets the call for another blockbuster film, he's ready. No question. No hesitation.

While you may not be striving to win an Academy Award, Will's mantra should be yours too. *For life.*

Staying ready means that you can answer the call. It means that regardless of how big or small the golden opportunity, you can rise to the occasion.

It's what gets—and keeps—you ready for the yes.

When you're ready for the yes, at a moment's notice you can:

- Fire off current marketing materials to promote your latest product or program on demand

- Finish a sales call and have a contract ready to be automatically delivered and signed once you close the deal

- Submit a proposal for a large contract

- Accept an offer to teach your live course for a group in your city, complete with curriculum and workbooks, within 72 hours

- Step up to a speaking engagement, collect the attendees' email addresses, and funnel those to a CRM for follow up

- Appear on a major network talk show, direct viewers to a website, and convert that traffic into cash

- Accept a great partnership opportunity that could really skyrocket your visibility and generate sales with the right product suite

- Provide a reporter with a bio, professional headshot, solid testimonials, and a copy of your latest book when you're contacted for a news feature

Do you have that media kit? Is your last photo shoot from your senior prom? Have you worked with enough clients to have fifteen glowing case studies or client success stories in your arsenal? Are your work and professional reputation so remarkable that someone wants to know your name? How boss are you—for real?

WHY MOST PEOPLE AREN'T READY FOR THE YES

If you answered "no" to any of the questions above, don't hit the freak-out button just yet. *Breathe.* You're in the right place. And you certainly are not alone.

There are a number of reasons why you weren't ready for your last big yes, whether the opportunity came to you or you went to it and got the cold shoulder:

You're getting advice from way too many people. We live in a world where we are overloaded with content. Everybody is a guru and offering you "25 Ways to Do This," and "75 Ways to Do That." You're following them all, confused, and picking up pieces of advice from each one as you go. Unsure who's who and what's what, you implement what all of these so-called business and branding "experts" tell you, hoping and praying that one day it will all come together and make sense. So you keep buying program after program, course after course, watching one free webinar after the other. You're all over the place and since you've hammered together your brand like a mad scientist, you now have an ugly, clunky Frankenstein on your hands. Your business is raggedy and limping. (And it shows.)

You've never experienced it. There haven't been enough micro "yesses" in your business to prepare you for the huge yes you've been waiting for. You've been working with clients for a few years now, but you're still treating your business as a hobby. Where are your contracts? Where is your proof that you delivered results? Who's talking about you? When you are really ready for the yes, you're always ready for any opportunity that comes your way.

You can't grab (and hold) attention. You have a little website, but it hasn't been updated in the last year. You have a good following on social media, but you're not engaging them with hot content.

In this world, you're competing against everything from the latest viral dance video to the last episode of *Empire*. People want to be constantly wowed, entertained, and informed. To get and keep eyes on you, you have to be interesting. You have to be doing or saying something remarkable. You have to be game changing enough to make your audience stop watching their favorite celebrity giving birth and say, "Okay, I need to talk to that person now." I know. It's cold outchea in these internet streets.

You aren't clear on what you're known for. One day you're a coach. The next day, you're a dog walker. The week after that you decide to dabble in a little fashion and open an online boutique. Now, why not sell waist trainers and teach women how to print their own t-shirts? It's okay to explore and experiment with your ideas and interests until you find the thing you truly love. But when you promote and talk about everything you're into, and want people to pay you for it, no one knows where to start.

How can someone say yes to you if they don't know what you're asking for?

Getting clear on what you want to be known for is the first step to building your personal brand. When you're solid on your expertise and offerings, other people will be too. Clarity makes it easy for people to talk about you and to refer you to others who may need you.

When there's a discussion about your industry, you want your name to be the first to come up in the conversation. If you become known as the best at what you do, the leader, the go-to guru that people can trust, you'll be more than popular—you'll be profitable.

Experts can command extremely high fees because of the demand for their services. Experts have their pick of the opportunities because people are lining up to hear what they have to say.

Experts get the yes. Every time. All the time.

WHAT'S AN EXPERT (AND HOW DO YOU BECOME ONE)?

By definition, an expert is someone who has a great deal of knowledge about, or skill, training, or experience in a particular field or activity.

This is certainly the respectable, proper, and buttoned-up response. My remix?

Someone who knows so much about a thing that whenever that thing is mentioned, no other name comes to mind but theirs.

One of my favorite experts is my mom. While she may not call herself an expert per se, she is, without a doubt, the best at cooking soul food. She's been the head of our family's kitchen for the last thirty years, can season chicken, greens, and gravy without even thinking about a measuring cup or a recipe, and everybody who has ever tasted anything she's cooked knows that she is the champ. There is no one who can come close to my mother in the kitchen.

Has she attended the Le Cordon Bleu or some other illustrious culinary school? No. Could she rival any soul food cook in the kitchen, publish a line of great cookbooks, and sit down with Ellen to have a deep conversation about the meaning of home-cooked meals and why every family needs them? Absolutely.

Expertise is book knowledge, formal study, and hands-on experience. You cannot legitimately call yourself an expert if you haven't tested what you've learned in the real world.

Wondering if you are a true expert? Here are some questions to ask yourself:

Do I have crazy experience doing something?

Have I been doing that thing for an extremely long time?

Do other people acknowledge me for it?

Can I have an intelligent, lengthy conversation with someone else in my industry about it?

If you are able to nod your head to all of the above, congratulations! You're officially reached expert status. Not bad. But now I have a deeper question for you.

Do you own it?

When you know you're an expert, your confidence is unshakable. You jump out of bed early and demand premium rates. You take what you do so seriously, that you live to be tested. You know that nobody can outshine you. When you're an expert, nobody can come for you. Ever. You will take on anybody, on any stage, anywhere, and at any time.

Now keep in mind, I didn't say you wouldn't be shaking in your shoes when you did it. Is there a chance you could get booed? Sure. Could you flop like you've never flopped before? Yup. But how will you know if you're not willing to step up there and try?

When you own your genius, you don't back down. If you get one shot, you throw on your Eminem sweater (you know the one with the vomit on it from Mom's spaghetti?), and you lose yourself in the moment. And after you crush it, and the crowd is rocking and chanting your name, your only question will be, "Man, I avoided all of this because I was scared? I just shut it down!"

That's what owning it looks like.

DON'T FAKE IT 'TIL YOU MAKE IT. PLEASE.

Not unlike a three-dollar bill, you can spot a fake expert from a mile away. Aside from shying away from a rap battle, they just don't have it all together. They may have all of the trappings of someone who should shine—the looks, bubbly personality, great graphics. But when you actually get up close and personal, there is nothing beneath the surface but a whole lotta s_____ (I'll let you fill in the blank).

Real experts talk the talk.

Think about if you pulled up to your favorite taco or burger spot. You're starving after a long day in the office without lunch and you've been dreaming about this meal all day. You have your mouth set for a grab-and-go hot meal that you can curl up on the couch with and catch the next episode of *Empire.* You place your initial order with the teenage kid with the big smile and you start to proceed down the line to add your toppings.

"I'll take onions, cheese, lettuce, and tomatoes, please."

"I'm sorry, ma'am," the cute girl who is building your burger says, "what's a tomato?"

Not quite the expertise you expected, is it?

Real experts walk the walk.

A few months ago, I attended a really big conference. There were two very well-known industry leaders there, both of whom paid a significant fee to speak. (We'll talk more about that later.) Well-known Dude A paid $100,000 to speak on the main stage and host a break-out session during the event weekend. Well-Known Dude B paid $30,000 for a keynote speaking spot. Interestingly, both presented at the exact same time. Can you guess whose session was packed?

You guessed it—Dude A.

His high-level investment spoke to his confidence in his expertise and his ability to teach and share it with his audience. Dude had that top-flight swag; his confidence was on ten, so he stroked a check that spoke to his belief in himself and what he could do. And it paid off.

When you know your stuff, you can invest at a higher level. You know you ain't going to lose. Just like with poker, you don't throw those cards down unless you're confident you have the winning hand.

Can you imagine how Dude B felt when ten people showed up in his room? I'd be willing to bet he flew home that weekend plotting on a master plan to get his weight up and crush that main stage next year.

If you are teetering on the edge of becoming an expert, know that, just like everything else in life, there are levels to this. Remember the $100K Dude and the $30K Dude that I mentioned earlier? Both of them were indeed experts, but one had the profits and the confidence to solidify who was the best in the room. Strive to be the $100K guy, but own your expertise right now, regardless of where you fall on the profit pole.

Start claiming it and establish yourself in one of these three ways:

- **Option One:** Master your thing. Get a real handle on what you do. Know it inside and out.

- **Option Two: Education and Research.** Read every book you can get your hands on. Invest in credible courses. Attend events and stay on top of industry changes online.

- **Option Three:** Do all of the above and get tons of hands-on experience.

CHAPTER TWO
HOW TO BE SEEN AS A PRO FROM THE START

Let's imagine, just for a moment, that you wake up tomorrow seriously sick. After tossing and turning for half the night, you call your primary care physician first thing in the morning, hoping for a last-minute appointment. She miraculously makes room for you, so you manage to throw a jacket over your pajamas, shuffle to the car, and make it to the office. Your doctor takes one good look at your swollen, sweaty face and calls a specialist who can see you right away.

As soon as you arrive at the next office (right before you pass out), a nurse quickly ushers you into an examination room. A few minutes later, a doctor comes in. Pushing his tortoise-shell glasses up on his nose, he extends a sweaty hand to you to shake. He definitely looks a little goofy and nervous, but you figure since he was recommended by another doctor that you trust, there's no need to panic—at least not yet.

He clears his throat and introduces himself.

"Hi, I am Doctor So-and-So. And I'm new."

Exit Stage Left.

There are few words in the English language that strike more fear in the hearts of your clients than "new." As soon as someone hears it, they shut down and nothing you say or do, from that moment on, can revive the confidence and belief that you can pull this thing off. All of your hard work, all of your experience, and all of the expertise that you know you can deliver goes out of the window. When you place yourself in the new category, the assumption is you don't have a clue about what you're doing, you lack confidence, and most importantly, if given the opportunity, the chances of you jacking something up is about as likely as an ice cube dissolving on a hot, sizzling sidewalk.

Just like you wouldn't want a new doctor learning on the job when it comes to your irreplaceable body, a new physical trainer teaching you how to get that body in shape, or the new person on fries handling your precious cheat-day fast food order, no one wants a newbie "expert" experimenting on their lives through the service or product that you offer. And they certainly don't want to pay you for it.

An "I'm new," from you almost always equals an automatic, "I'm a no," from your potential client.

But can we get real for a minute?

Are you *really* new at this? Or are you simply worried that you don't measure up? Are you comparing yourself to someone else's business that appears to be at level one hundred and feeling like yours is at level zero? (Guess they didn't start from nowhere, huh?) Are you questioning if you truly have what it takes?

So here's the real question:

Are you a newbie or are just showing up like one?

I'm going to go out on a limb here and guess that your standard, "Hi, I'm New," introduction is really a cop out. It's an easy and convenient way for you not to be as great as you know you should be—as great as you could be—if you would just show up.

You are giving yourself permission to screw up.

You are justifying those weak, hand-me-down graphics and images.

You want to convince yourself that no one will listen to you.

You are playing small.

When you hide behind your newness, you are not only talking yourself out of business, but you are also discounting everything you've done and invested in getting here. That includes all of the work you've finished for free or for less than what you should have charged. It includes all of the courses, the classes, and the books you've bought and read. You've earned the right to be here. No, you're not new at all. Not by a long shot.

You're scared.

The reality is that with a big adjustment to your confidence and a few (okay, more like thirty) tweaks to your brand and how you show up, you too can go from zero to one hundred. *Real quick.*

WHEN YOU SHOW UP, SHOW ALL THE WAY OUT

When it comes to entering the market for the first time, there are, indeed, levels to this. If you want to be seen, respected, and paid like the expert you are, every aspect of your personal brand must scream top-flight. It is essential that your brand—and anything that represents it—looks and feels well-polished and organized. (That's everything, including you.)

Keep in mind that showing up as if you are (insert the PG-13 rating here) *the shit*, will impact and drive everything about your business. The types of speaking and partnership opportunities that come your way. The clients who respond to your marketing and book consultations. The press and media who take interest in you—and your money.

The people who show up in the market as pros get paid like pros. End of story. Show me someone who is struggling to keep their business profitable, get clients in the door, or gain a foothold in the market, and I'll show you a raggedy brand.

Here's the bottom line—now that you've owned that you are an expert and you've claimed the confidence to back it up, it's essential that you look like it.

You've heard the saying that you only have one chance to make a first impression, right? As overused as that cliché is, it hasn't been around since Moses wore short pants for a reason. The idea that you need to come of out of the gate swinging—hard— is tried, tested, and true in every aspect of life, including with your personal brand.

We'll discuss and dig deeper into these elements as we move through the book, but when it comes to elevating your brand to pro status, here are some key areas to consider:

Website

Your website is, in most instances, someone's first real glimpse of you and your business. When Google leads that blind date (also known as a potential client) there, you want it to be love at first site (pun intended). This is your online home, your digital storefront, so anything less than incredible is unacceptable.

Images

Professional images are an absolute must. Every photo of you that officially represents your brand should speak the right language and uphold the Holy Grail of Branding—professional, personable, and premium. Selfies are fine to share casually on social, but your photos on your website, marketing material, and products should be beautifully branded.

Contracts

As you build out the various workflows needed to support your business, you'll determine what forms you'll need to have on hand. But one of those, without a doubt, will be contracts. You should always have fillable contracts on hand for each service, ready to roll out of your inbox at the tap of a button. In addition to alerting the world that you mean serious business, sound contracts will protect you and your business should a client relationship, partnership or collaboration go downhill. #dontgetburned

Social Media

They don't call it social for no reason. Your social media pages and platforms are your golden opportunity to really engage and interact with the people who will pay you. Show up; be social and consistent both with your visuals and content.

Collaborations and Relationships

"Is that her, *again*?" Have you ever caught yourself asking that very question about someone in your industry who seems to be everywhere, all the time?

Well, while you may consider it to be overkill or overexposure, the truth is the person who shows up the most is typically the one who gets the shot. Does that mean they are the most credentialed or qualified? Not necessarily. But everybody knows them and that's the person who's thought of when it comes time to make the deal. They were at the right place at the right time. High visibility pays off.

When you are regularly seen at industry events and make an effort to get to know other people there, you'll start to establish mutually beneficial relationships. People will want to get to know you and what you do.

So while you're shading that chick on Instagram who manages to attend every hot networking event in the city while you scroll from the couch, give it a try. Make an appearance at the right events. Get out and meet some people that you can build with. Don't hate, participate.

Content

Create content that sells for you. Look for problems and frustrations that you can fix and solve them with your content. For example, when I first came on the scene, I would get so many clients who were hesitant to invest in professional graphic design services, so they wanted to try it on their own. I would do my best to educate them, even warn them, about the headaches and pitfalls of DIY, but there were some daredevils who insisted they could do it. Instead of continuing to invest my energy in attempting to sell my services to people who may or may not be a good fit, I decided to create a video that discussed the advantages and disadvantages of hiring a graphic designer versus going the DIY route. Instead of doing all of the talking with individual people, I allowed that video to do it for me. It positioned me as an expert and was very effective in drawing the right client to me—the one who saw the value in my service and was willing to invest to get it.

THE PRICE HAS GOT TO BE RIGHT

(IF YOU PLAN ON STAYING IN BUSINESS)

If you've experienced me on any platform—from Facebook to Periscope to my local grocery store—you know that pricing your services and products is one of my favorite topics. While a conversation about pricing may seem premature before the other elements of your brand are in place or even out of place in a book about personal branding, the fact is, it isn't. It's never too early to talk about money.

You are in business, right?

Frankly, it's impossible to discuss the importance of showing up like a pro without addressing the cost that you attach to what you do and sell. Your prices are actually one of the most the important pieces of your profitable brand plan. What you charge says so much about your business before you open your mouth to say a word. So you have to make sure that your prices speak the right language and convey the right message about what you offer.

More than a conversation about dollars and cents, pricing is about value. What value do you bring to the market and to your client's experience? How much is your time and expertise worth? If you perceive your offerings to be valuable, you have to price them accordingly.

Prices that are way below the market standard are red flags.

Low pricing, more often than not, is a sign of someone who does not value their offerings. In addition to that, low pricing is typically associated with poor quality. The thing about bargain pricing is that it not only sheds a bad light on your business but muddies your entire industry. Like that no-name, drug store perfume or cologne, cheap prices will grab attention, but not for the right reasons. Cheap reeks of limitation and fear.

And nothing smells funkier than desperation.

***** And For Now a Public Service Announcement*****

Attention Ladies, Ladies, Ladies—this message is for you.

Many women find it challenging to see the value in what they bring to the table. We tend to undervalue ourselves in any scenario that involves business and money—be it in the workplace or our own companies. Women shy away from conversations about their worth and find it hard to demand what they deserve. Meanwhile, your cut-to-the-chase, but underqualified male peer is closing the deals and getting the promotions. Why? Because he has the balls to ask for it.

Here are a few more reasons why you shouldn't be the cheapest kid on the block:

- **You're cheating yourself out of what you deserve.** This goes back to worth. When you've put in the work, your pricing should correlate to your investment in yourself and in your business. As an expert, you deserve to earn a premium rate to provide a premium service and experience for your clients. Period.

- **You're not holding your client responsible for their investment.** People show up according to what they have at stake. The higher the price tag that is associated with the experience or the result, the more effort is put into the outcome. Your client will have a better appreciation for your work and theirs when the price isn't too low. Someone who invests $30,000 for a business coach likely is going to show up and grind much harder than someone who invested $300.00.

- **You will finish how you start.** While it is not impossible to raise your prices as your business grows (and in some instances, you should) it is a challenge. Once the market sees you as cheap, that's what they'll expect forever. Think about how you would react if you pulled up to your local dollar store to find that the prices were now on par with Target or a high-end retailer. Would you shop there or would it make more sense just to bounce to that other store and get the complete experience? If you start out playing small, chances are you'll stay stuck there.

YOU ARE WHAT YOU INVEST

If you are shaking in your boots at the thought of charging

anything above $100.00 for your services, chances are you have not invested enough in your development as an entrepreneur. The rule is you have to spend with others in the same way and at the same level you want people to spend with you. Investing in yourself and your business at a premium level will give you a completely new perspective on pricing and the expectations that come along with a higher price point. You can't possibly imagine receiving five figures in your account from a client if you've never paid it to someone else. At the same time, you'll get the benefit of what a high-end program or product can offer you.

Lastly, once you've made a significant investment in your business, your confidence will be on ten. Personally, I've invested over $50,000 in my business over the last three years. That amount is nothing to sneeze at, but it was worth every dime since I've made it back several times over as a result of what I took from those courses, conferences, and even books. Not to mention, now that I've crossed that investment threshold, I don't bat an eyelash when I present my prices to a client. I'm worth it. And you are too.

SETTING YOUR PRICES

Since we've talked at length about what not to do, let's discuss how to approach pricing in your business. As you are developing your price structure, think about this:

- **Set some boundaries.** In business, time is money. As your business grows, you'll have less bandwidth, so implementing a break point between you and potential clients is very important. One of the easiest ways to do this is to create a form for anyone who is interested in your services to complete. Determine how serious they are. Qualify the opportunity before setting an appointment or picking up the phone.

- **Go big.** Here's a golden rule for pricing—if you say a number without stuttering, it's not big enough. **Your premium prices should scare the shit out of you.** If they don't, go back to the pricing board. Increase until the amount doesn't just roll off your tongue anymore. Imagine a number so huge that you would rather write it down on a cocktail napkin and slide it across a table like they do in the movies. If you can envision your client's eyes bugging out of their heads when they open it, you've got it.

I have a famous test that I run on Periscope to see how comfortable people are when quoting prices. I start with a low number, let's say $100.00, and I ask people if they are comfortable asking clients or customers for that investment. And I keep increasing the amount in increments of one hundred, so I go from $100.00 to $200.00 to $300.00, and so forth. I typically get a lot of people who say, "Yeah, I can ask for that!" until I get to the $500.00 mark. That's when people start to get nervous. Their insecurities start to show up *big time*. So when I jump it up to $2000.00, I lose people. Then I take it up by a few more thousand. By then, almost all of my viewers have bailed.

Always remember that it's them, it's not you. Set your prices and stand behind them.

DON'T BLOCK YOUR FLOW (OR YOUR DOUGH)

Your energy around money shows up everywhere—in your sales calls, your proposals, and any inquiry you respond to about your prices. Don't bring your personal money blocks to your business. When you are scared of money or you operate from a space of broke as opposed to a space of wealth, you'll feel guilty about pricing as if you're stealing from people or causing them hardship because of a business transaction.

If you make the assumption (which is often wrong) that people cannot afford you, you will constantly feel compelled to discount your services and you'll never build the profitable business you've dreamed about.

Free yourself from any negativity around money so you can earn what you deserve.

SOMETIMES A PRO HAS TO TAKE IT SLOW

I know—you've been fired up and ready to go hard with your business for quite some time now. Maybe you've had this idea simmering inside of you for a while, you've dabbled with a few brave friends or people you know to get your feet wet, and now you're ready to get serious. Or maybe you've been in full-fledged business and you're ready to step your game up. And all of this scary talk about big brands and big money that we've had so far hasn't scared you one bit. In fact, you're even more pumped than you were before. You're ready to jump. Before you grab that parachute...

Hold up, wait a minute.

Showing up in the market as a true pro may mean that you have to do a little more prep work first. It's okay to check yourself before you wreck yourself; in fact, that's exactly what you want to do. You want to see how you can really diversify what you do and where there are opportunities to challenge the norm, which is really where the growth is.

Here are a few more considerations worth mentioning:

You could save time. Moving slowly and strategically into your business idea allows you to test the idea and the market before going all in. You'll get to determine if this is really the thing you want to do and be known for. You can also see if this is something that can really work outside of your head and in the world with the people you really want to work with. Assess the land before you get too far away from the shore and into the deep end of the ocean.

You could save money. If the thing you thought was a sure thing turns out to not be the thing at all, it's best to know before you invest that $15,000 in graphic design and branding.

You could save face. Easing into business gives you the chance and the grace to learn the ropes a bit, test the waters, and *fix* your stuff before the whole world (also known as Facebook) sees it and burns you at the digital stake. Not to mention you'll have to tell your Momma that you flopped. (Her opinion still matters.)

You will save your ass. See all of the above.

FAILING IS NORMAL, SO EXPECT IT

So here's the deal, Love. (Have you noticed that I only call you that when I am about to drop a bomb on you? If you didn't, now my cover is blown. But it's okay. I still love you.) Now for that bomb.

Despite the fact that you want to do everything you possibly can to avoid anything going wrong, it will. Failing is part of the process and while it is natural to have an aversion to it, you shouldn't. Business is a game, and just like with anything else, the smaller the risk, the smaller the reward.

Instead of embracing a mindset that runs from failure, decide that you are going to expect it. If you know there is a chance that you'll flop and you're willing to fail, you won't take it personally when (not if) it happens. Failures don't always have to be catastrophic. You may not lose your life savings, but you may lose a client or launch a product that you love and the world hates and refuses to buy. You may make ten sales calls and not close one or try your first Facebook ad campaign with an investment of a few hundred dollars and not reap anything from it.

It's okay.

The key is to dust yourself off and try again. And again. And *again*. You keep doing it, keep tweaking it, keep trying it, until you get it right.

Most people don't get it right, not because it didn't work, but because they gave up too damn soon. You cannot go into business expecting instant results or for something to work perfectly the first time out—even when you take a huge risk to make it happen. A single large investment in a coach or a course or a degree may not be your claim to fame and fortune. One book (even this amazing one you're reading right now) is not going to have all of the answers to guarantee your success.

Anyone who has ever done anything big in this life has failed at least once before getting to that one big win. People like Oprah, Walt Disney, J.K. Rowling, and Stephen King all know what it's like to fail.

Failure doesn't care how many degrees you have, how many times you were nice to your pain-in-the-royal ass neighbor, or that fact that you did exactly what your Momma told you to do by graduating and getting a great job. Shit happens—in life and in business. And when it does, it will always leave a lesson behind. Your job is to pick it up and learn it.

Your life has been influenced by more than one person, and your millions will be cultivated by more than one thing. Learn from everyone, even their mistakes. And always learn from your own. Be willing to fail. If you aren't, you've lost before you even started.

When you do, the success is so much sweeter.

Failing is not a bad thing, *at all*. Believe it or not, it could be the best thing that happens to you.

Part Two

PREPARING FOR THE YES!

CHAPTER THREE

AS SEEN IN...

Every superstar, regardless of who they are, needs a stage. Now, that stage could be a stadium filled to capacity with hundreds of thousands of people; a dark, smoky nightclub for a small, intimate crowd; or a theater—but it's a stage none-theless.

A stage is the place where a superstar shines. It's where they do their thing, and when they step onto it, everybody stops and listens. A stage is where they kill it. Rip it. *Own it.*

And that's exactly why you need one.

As an expert in your space, you need a stage—a platform—to share your expertise and shine a light on your brilliance. Getting in front of people, *consistently and constantly*, and telling them what you do and how you do it is essential to establishing a profitable personal brand. When an audience sees and hears you speaking, presenting, and teaching on a topic, it automatically gives them a sense of confidence. It allows them to see themselves as the person on the receiving end of your knowledge and all that you know. It helps them to see what you can do for them.

And that is what makes people want to buy from you.

So, yes, it's time to grab those big girl drawers and get in front of the world.

A STAGE IS A STAGE, BABY

Keep in mind that a platform doesn't always mean sharing your expertise from a stage or even in front of a large crowd. While live events that offer you the chance to hone your speaking skills and grow your brand are great opportunities, a platform only really needs two things:

Number One: You sharing information out for someone to hear.

A platform could be your website where you share industry insight. It could be your blog or podcast where you share informational tidbits on how someone could improve one thing in their life or business today. A platform could also be your social media page that is devoted to your personal per-spective on business and current events. It all qualifies and counts. You are sharing information, and now all you need is the second element of a platform:

Number Two: A person who is there to hear the informa-tion that you share.

And that one person that shows up? That is your audience. It's not the size of the crowd; it's the power of your content that counts. Regardless of whether your crowd count remains at one or balloons to one million, you always have one job—to deliver. This is a stage, your stage, (even when you may be sharing it with someone else) so when that mic is passed to you, you have a responsibility to set it on fire. The key to commanding your platform is to show up and show out—each and every time.

Because you never know who's watching.

Whether it's your first big client or your first client ever in life, it's always a possibility that the opportunity could come your way as a result of someone having a direct experience with you on a platform. We live in a world where there are eyeballs everywhere, all the time. People have access to you and your voice at the click of a button or an app. As soon as you hit record on your video or post that content, someone is right there, waiting, ready to make a decision about you and what you can do.

If you rock it out and it's love at first look or listen, maybe they'll come back for more. But let's pretend, just for a second that this is it. You've got this one chance to show them that you know your 'ish. Do you really want to waste it? Do you want to think about what you could be missing if you decide not to kill it on that stage today?

Do you think Justin Beiber knew on the day that he sang his baby blond-haired heart out that a mega record executive would spot him on YouTube?

Do you think Kevin Hart knew when he got laughed off the stage in his early career that he would become one of the highest-paid comedians of this decade, snatching up block-buster movie deals and MAJOR endorsements?

Do you think when Tyler Perry came out on the stage and poured his all into those Madea shows that he knew it would result in millions upon millions of coins and fans?

You do have something to say and to show too. You do have something that you want the world to know about so you can sell it to the people it can help and serve. You have an expertise and a talent that can only be delivered the way you bring it.

You are in business, right?

So your stage may be a stadium filled with thousands of people or your very first Facebook Live when only your best friend pops on and beats the hell outta that Love button. Your stage could be a small group workshop in your area or an online virtual summit with a group of industry peers. The point is that how the platform presents itself isn't nearly as important as how you show up on it.

You show up like this is the audition of all auditions.

You show up like this is your one and only shot.

You show up like the biggest YES of your life.

And when all else fails, you show up like you're six years old, it's after-Christmas dinner shenanigans in Grandma's living room, and your momma puts you on the spot to remind everyone that *her* kid is the star of *this* family. The moment you've been waiting for. You grab your favorite gift of the year, that plastic microphone from Santa (you know the one that's attached to its own speaker) and blow. That's right, you get 'em, baby.

Because a stage is a stage. All day, every day.

SOMETIMES YOU GOTTA BUILD YOUR OWN

AND IT'S OKAY

Before I launched my branding agency, I had a pretty dope photography studio in Memphis, Tennessee. That was my first business—my first baby—and I ate and slept the business of photography. Visuals, in some shape or form, have always been my thing, a piece of my genius, so I loved everything about taking photos and capturing people and places through my lens.

As my company grew and I explored the local photography and arts community more, I started to connect with more and more local artists. Some were photographers, but there were also artists, muralists, musicians, singers, you name it. Any medium that had an artistic component to it, there was someone in Memphis using it and striving to earn a living in the process. It was like I'd discovered a whole new world that I didn't know existed—this crankin' underground of creatives who all wanted any and everybody to know about their work.

And that's when it hit me. I realized there was no real place for creatives to showcase their work. Memphis wasn't really known for its arts and culture, so there really wasn't a mainstream art world. Outside of a few musical monuments honoring the blues that the city was known for, there were few art exhibits, events, or places where artists could be seen by residents or each other. Some of us had been featured in a newspaper here and there, but that was about the extent of the exposure. Few people outside of our clients and customers knew we existed, much less anyone outside of Memphis. The more creatives I met, the more obvious it became that we were all wanting and needing the same thing—eyeballs on our work.

A few of us had stepped out there and pitched ourselves to publications, but most of us were just doing great work and hoping that somebody would eventually take notice. The bottom line was we were waiting for a shot at a stage, and that shot may or may not have ever come, regardless of how phenomenal we were.

That's when something else hit me. We needed to think outside of snatching somebody else's stage. We needed to create something that belonged to us. We needed a platform.

So my first magazine, Love Nu Art, was born.

Once I got the idea, it was off to the races. I started collaborating with other artists and photographing their work. I was taking these incredible images and I wanted as many people as possible to see them, so I decided to publish this digital glossy magazine that grew from a figment of my imagination to real, beautiful pages. The magazine became so popular that we created a series of events to expand the experience, and what was supposed to be just a few artists getting together for performances and a celebration of the latest issue became one of the city's hottest happenings. People loved what we were doing and finally our creative community started to get the shine it deserved. Our businesses and audiences grew and, for the first time, some artists were able to see their work in print. It was, by far, one of the most amazing things I've ever done in my life.

While many people thought I created Love Nu Art because I wanted to be a baby Oprah and share my million-dollar Kool-Aid smile on the front of my own magazine (don't get me wrong—there is nothing wrong with that), it was about more than that, just like it is for her. I really needed a place and a space to do what I wanted to do. I wanted to let my creativity and my vision run wild, to say what I wanted to say and show what I wanted to show. I wanted the freedom of owning my own thing.

Now I am in no way knocking mainstream publications, major networks, and popular platforms because we all need those shots at the "big time" to expand our reach and our business. In fact, many of us dream of being "good enough" to get a call from a top-rated talk show, radio show, or a magazine that graces newsstands. But often those opportunities come with a sacrifice. When you are invited to a stage of that magnitude, you may have to agree to show up as a less-risky, more universal (also known as watered down) version of yourself. You may be asked to tailor yourself and your message to suit a particular agenda or audience. If you're not considered to be "polished" enough, the producer may need to spit-shine you up a bit. Cue the stiff smile and the BS. Is that something you can feel good about?

When you own your platform, you get to make the rules. You ultimately get to decide how creative you want to be. You get to determine what you say and how. You don't need permission from a third-party and you and your team (even if it's just a team of one—you) get to set the tone for how you deliver what you do.

Ownership is power. Ownership is respect. And ownership is money. If you want to control the flow of all of those things in your business, you have to be willing to step out and build your own stage if you have to.

What it really boils down to is this:

Everybody is not going to get your vision, and that's cool.

In fact, it's damn cool, because it means that you get to do it the way nobody else has done it. And that is never, *ever*, a bad thing.

PLATFORM POSSIBILITIES

When it comes to the platforms that you can create, the sky is almost the limit. There are so many ways for you to get in front of people to share your knowledge. Here are some of my favorites to get you started:

- Live Streaming

- Vlogging

- Podcasting

- Speaking (create your own event or as a guest of another host)

- Webinars

- Tele-classes

- Online and Offline Events

As you are deciding which opportunity to jump on or launch first, here are some key questions to ask yourself:

How do I show up best? You want to pick a platform that's comfortable for you. If you don't want to be seen on video, then creating a podcast would be ideal. If you feel like your voice sucks, then maybe you want to focus on writing, creating, and publishing content, which takes your voice out of people's heads. Don't allow an area where you still need to grow hinder you from progress. You may decide to work with a vocal coach or speaker trainer down the road so you can get more comfortable with your voice (or just suck it up and get out there like I did) but in the meantime, play your strengths.

Where can I get the most visibility? Think about the reach of the platforms that you're considering. You want to choose platforms that are timeless and have what I like to call legendary status. Don't always limit yourself to one thing and/or only what's trendy at the time. Instead, think about the platforms that won't go out of style, at least not anytime soon. Social media is great, and I love it, but don't place all of your time and energy eggs in one basket. Your favorite feed could be here today and gone tomorrow, so you still want to maintain a website.

Also, pick platforms that have the best distribution channels. If you do a podcast, you can syndicate it through iTunes, Stitcher, iHeartRadio, Google Play, Apple TV, SoundCloud, and just like that, you have at least seven distribution channels from creating one form of media. You want something with a high distribution aspect.

What is popular right now? Consider what people are using all of the time. Live streaming has become really hot and more mainstream. The world is so used to it that streaming video has now become a part of our culture and more people are jumping on board every day. And while it seems like a bit of a fad now, it's likely that streaming will be here, in some form, for the foreseeable future. Streaming is a great way to get in front of people in real time, so hopping on a platform like Facebook Live makes sense. Keep an eye out for the platforms that are drawing a crowd and become an early adopter when you can.

Do I understand it? It's always best to choose platforms that you know how to use. If you are considering Periscope, for example, practice a bit on your own before people seek you out and follow you. Do you know how to flip the camera around so viewers see your face and not your floor while you fumble with your phone? Can you tell people which icons to hit to give hearts or invite followers to view your broadcast? Know how to use the platform, the technology, and how to leverage it first.

Keep in mind that people will always remember what you show them first. If you suck on your first webinar, the likelihood of the same people showing up a second time is minimal to none. Think about when you go to a new restaurant for the first time. You may be all excited to try it, but as soon as you walk in, it's one disaster after another. After you've waited at the door for twenty-five minutes without so much as a glance from one of the ten staff who've passed you, the greeting that you finally get from the host is filed to the brim with attitude. As you follow him to the table, you notice the place is filthy. Your server takes her sweet time making her way to take your order, and when she does, your meal is all wrong.

With all of this disorganization, what is the likelihood that you'll give this dump another chance to snatch your hard-earned money? The people who decide to spend their precious time to show up to hear or to see you are just like you as a consumer. They may not have spent money with you, yet, but your audience wants the best you have to offer, so don't waste their time. Like it or not, you are a star.

So give the people what they want.

NOW WE CAN SEE YOU

By now, you've stuck that pinky toe in the water and given an audience a glimpse of who you are. Perhaps you chose a platform, and just for fun and out of curiosity, gave it a try. You may have just gotten in front of a few Facebook friends, but that's a start. You may be still feeling this whole visibility thing out a bit and getting comfortable with putting yourself out there.

But guess what? Somebody out there has seen how fantastic you are, and now they want more.

Or you may be like many entrepreneurs and you've put yourself out there, but nobody is showing up. Or you've been gaining some traction with a platform you've created, but when you get people in the room—live or virtually—you give them all you got once, but you have nothing else to hold them or to create that relationship that will ultimately lead to the sale.

The missing piece?

A personal brand.

Stepping out onto a stage is really just the beginning. While many business owners believe that getting in front of people is the be-all-end-all to profits, it really is just the beginning. You may get people in the room, but if you show up weak or unprepared to do real, legit business, all of your effort goes down the drain. When your personal brand is strong, and all of your ducks are in a row, you will demand the attention— and keep it.

You want to wow people with the website. You want to capture them with your content and valuable knowledge that you've published. You want to show up at the right events with the right people. You want products that make dollars and make sense. And you want the media chasing you to talk about it!

You want, and need, a profitable personal brand. Stick with me and I will show you everything you need to build one.

A profitable personal brand is all about positioning yourself for that yes that is certainly headed your way. When you have all of the elements like visuals, published content, speaking

engagements, programs, and products, you move from struggling entrepreneur into a new level. Boss.

You begin to attract the right opportunities as opposed to
scouring the earth looking for scraps. You get to choose
what you want to do and who you want to work with. You
have the confidence that it takes to command the respect
and the revenue that your expertise deserves. It's all possible
when your name not only becomes recognizable but, most
importantly, is synonymous with excellence and quality.

Remember, your name is worth millions.

So are you gonna talk about it or be about it?

Your personal brand is the full representation of how you
show up in the market. Everything we've talked about until
this point—owning your expertise, cementing your confidence, and opening yourself to the sometimes scary, but always worth it, necessity of being seen and heard—has been
gearing you up for the work you'll need to put in to create a
phenomenal and profitable personal brand.

Before we move any further, I have to say this.

Disclaimer: You will hate me before you love me...again.

You may have concluded by now that I am a no-nonsense
kinda girl. So I can't bojangle you. This is about to be some
serious work. As you move through the rest of these pages,
I may not be your friend in your head for a while, and that's

okay. I can take it. Because I know everything we're about to do here is worth it.

I know you're worth it.

I wrote this book because I don't want to just see you do just any 'ol thing. I want to see you do some shit that is out of this world. I want to see you crush it. I want to see you win. So I am showing up. And I hope that you will too.

Don't rush through this process. Take your time. Give it beyond the best that you thought you were yesterday. Spend the money. Invest in doing the work in each of these phases so that you can build something solid, something real. This is not about checking the box. This is about you hitting the ground running with a brand that is more extraordinary, more kick-ass, and more dope than the world has ever seen. This is about building the legacy you've always wanted to leave, to finally get those clients and those shots that you've been dreaming about. This is about creating something that you can say, with confidence, "Yeah! I did that." This is about getting everything that seemed so far out of your reach—until today.

That is what I want for you.

Now, let's do this work.

THE SEVEN PHASES OF YOUR PROFITABLE

PERSONAL BRAND

The Seven Phases of a Profitable Personal Brand is my incredible signature system for building your brand from the ground up. It is designed to be comprehensive, addressing each of the elements that you'll need to jumpstart your brand presence.

The phases are like building blocks and each one includes a specific set of activities for you to complete and leverage as you move from one phase to the next. As you implement each phase, you'll begin to see your personal brand take shape and other people will take notice.

Do it right, and you'll see the results.

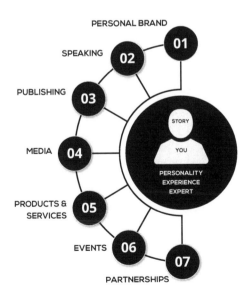

CHAPTER FOUR

ME: INCORPORATED: HOW TO BUILD A PERSONAL BRAND

Denzel Washington. Tom Hanks. Halle Berry. Queen Latifah.

You may be familiar with each of these celebrities based on what they do for a living, the companies they own, and the products they endorse, but what you really see at work are their personal brands. Each of them has become known for something—be it their hard-core work ethic, humor, glamor, good looks—or a combination of personal and professional qualities. Their reputations have become attached to their names, so when someone mentions them, something instantly clicks.

When you hear Denzel or Tom as a moviegoer, you know to grab your popcorn, sit back, and expect (usually) a really good film that will leave you feeling something.

When you hear Halle or Latifah as a producer, a casting agent, or a cosmetics company, you know to not pick up the phone unless you have a multi-million dollar budget. *B**ch betta have their money.*

Tom Hanks is that goofy uncle that can make you laugh or cry at the drop of a hat while Latifah is that always-down best friend who can go from snatch-off-these-earrings to red-carpet glamor in a heartbeat. The point is that there is something, based on how they show up on screen and in your life, you like, or maybe don't, about each of them as people. You either love or hate them based on what they represent.

And all of that emotion is driven by each of their names.

One of the first things that make these actors so popular and powerful in Hollywood is the weight of their names. Their names have become their currency, so much so that they are paid insane amounts of money for just stepping on set or at an event in anticipation of the results they are expected to produce. They've shown up so consistently, performed so well, and mastered their craft to a point that they've placed a stamp on our culture. They've each erected a legacy that will last far beyond their lifetimes.

Your name has power.

And that's why you have to lead with it and define it for the world.

YOUR NAME IS YOUR MOST VALUABLE ASSET

"Except my name. I'll give up all that other stuff, but only if I get to keep my name. I've worked too hard for it, your honor."

In that famous courtroom scene from *What's Love Got to Do With It?* Angela Bassett, who portrayed the beast that is Tina Turner, proclaimed those words to the judge during her divorce proceedings. She walked away from potentially millions of dollars, property, diamonds, and furs for one thing—her name. She had cried, danced, chanted, and Proud Mary-ed every letter of that name. And she didn't want to lose the power or the profit (let's be real) that she knew was attached to it.

Your name, and all of the work that you've done to elevate and make it mean something, deserves to be preserved and protected.

That is why your name is the foundation of your personal brand.

Building a personal brand around your name is one of the smartest things you can do as an entrepreneur. Why? I am so glad you asked.

It's the one thing that nobody can take from you. Let's be honest, business and money can be snatched out from under you. You could lose all of your material possessions (shirt included) tomorrow. But, your name, in the words of Ike Turner, "stays home."

It's distinct. Denzel, now and forever. There is only one him, and there is only one you. (Even if there is some alien out there with the exact same first name and last name, chances are there is a spelling or a middle initial that you can use to distinguish yourself. If not, that would just be freaky, and means that you should probably give your momma a call, like right now.)

It's something you can grow with. A company will come and go. Your audience, products, and even your interests will too. When you create a personal brand based on your name, you can be fluid and explore new ideas and meet the needs and demands of your clients as they evolve.

Keep in mind that while your personal brand should lead, that doesn't mean that a creative company name that complements your personal brand cannot follow. You will find some people, like Oprah, who operate as a personal brand nearly one-hundred percent of the time when engaging with the market and then you have celebrities, like Richard Branson from Virgin, who play more behind the scenes of their companies. You can do both.

If you haven't started a company yet, this is the perfect time to allow the world to get to know you. Introduce them to your expertise and personality first, and then use your personal brand to anchor the company that you'll eventually create. If you have an existing company, now is the time to come out from the shadows with a personal brand that allows you to establish the real relationships that you need to grow.

Besides, when was the last time you saw a logo or a laptop speaking from a stage? Exactly.

WWW.YOU.COM

In the online world, owning your name starts with the domain. Think of your domain as the digital address for your website.

It's how people hit you up when they want to find you.

Before some sneaky cyber creep snatches it, run over to **www.godaddy.com** and purchase your name to ensure that **www.yourname.com** belongs to you. I recommend GoDaddy since they have 24/7 customer service and their long-standing reputation as a great company counts. I also recommend them for web hosting. You can purchase your domains for as low as $10.00 and you can find coupon codes out there to discount the standard rates.

Once you've secured yourname.com, you should consider purchasing other extensions like .live and .me for future web-sites that you may want to create as a secondary spin-off to your primary personal brand site.

WHO ARE YOU? LIKE FOR REAL?

Once you own your name, the next step to establishing your personal brand is to determine what your expertise is and what you want the world to know you for. This is all about the niche, and creating a lane that nobody can speed in but you. You really want to hone in on what you do—that thing that nobody else on this earth can do but you.

You have to get in touch with your core and ask yourself some real questions.

From this moment on, you can't simply be a coach, or a

designer, or a consultant. You need to be able to go deeper and decide what you really want to be when you grow up. Not for the applause and acclaim. Not for the money. Not for Moms. For you.

As you get into this, ask yourself:

- What do you *really* want to do?

- What do you want to be known for?

- What is your personality type?

Assess Yourself

Self-paced, personality-based assessments are an ideal way to get to know yourself so that you can more thoroughly and honestly answer some of these critical questions. I love these data-driven, comprehensive reviews that cover everything from leadership style to interpersonal skills. Believe it or not, all of your personal and professional traits play a big part in how you show up in business and what platforms, opportunities, clients, and even the types of content are best suited to you.

Are you meant to be the everything in your business or do you need a team to handle tasks while you focus on the vision? Should you work with clients 1:1 or are group programs better for you? How are you at sales? Are you an introvert or an extrovert? These are all extremely important as you are structuring your brand and your business.

By taking the time to do this work and get these answers up front, you can avoid falling into the trap of building a business that is everything that you *don't* want it to be.

If you've never done these assessments, now is the time.

Here are my personal favorites:

Kolbe Indexes: http://kolbe.com/assessments/

These quick tests are all about instinct and how you naturally do things. You'll learn how to leverage your instinctual talents to be most effective and productive.

How to Fascinate: http://www.howtofascinate.com/

Creator Sally Hogshead has developed this in-depth personality test to show you how to lead with your best traits. By understanding how the world already sees you, you'll learn how to work a room and a conversation like a superstar.

StrengthsFinder 2.0: http://strengths.gallup.com/default.aspx

This one is legendary. It's a little lengthy, but you'll walk away with some key insights into your core strengths and the professional opportunities that are best for you.

Entrepreneurial Profile 10: http://www.gallup.com/products/170990/entrepreneurial-profile.aspx

Are you about delegation or building relationships to get

things done? How do you show up in high-risk situations or when it's time to challenge the status quo? You'll know when you finish this assessment that is all about discovering your entrepreneurial talents.

VISUALLY SPEAKING

Before anyone reads your bio or goes to your website, they've likely had a peek at your brand identity somehow, somewhere. Your brand identity includes the elements—your logo, brand colors, brand patterns, fonts, photos—that show up for your personal brand.

Your brand identity is what gives people their first glimpse of you and really shapes their idea of what they can expect from their experience with you.

People have to be visually attracted to you first. Everything else is secondary.

Your brand identity is no different from dating, really. If you meet someone on the street, before they can open their mouth, you've sized them up based on their looks. Are the clothes tattered and cheap? The shoes scuffed? The knuckles and elbows ashy? All of these are visual and speak to how well you think the person cares about themselves (which could be a sign of how cheap they'd be on a date) or if you are one to go *alllll* the way there, how they would ultimately take care of you. Could you be potentially missing out on getting to know a really great person? Sure. But, let's be honest, is it likely that you'll look past what you see to find out? I'll let you keep that answer to yourself. (No judgment here.)

When your brand is visually raggedy, your potential clients question whether or not you are capable of taking good care of them and giving them a premium experience. It doesn't matter how phenomenal you are—if they can't sense that without speaking to you, you've lost the opportunity.

So step back from your brand (if you have one) or think about what you *thought* about doing before you picked up this phenomenal piece of work:

- When you put your graphics out here, what will people say?

- Does it look like you went with a low-cost freelance site or a hired a pro?

- What type of visuals are you creating?

- What type of content are you creating?

- What does your online presence look like?

- What does your social media presence look like? Are you active on your pages and posting content regularly, or are you ghost for months at a time?

- Do you look ready for the YES?

If there is anything remotely raggedy about your responses, you want to take a moment and assess how you can get this thing together. All of these things speak volumes about your brand so you want them right and tight. You want to attract and draw the right type of client to you, and your brand identity is one of the easiest ways to do that.

Let's go back to our Hollywood hitters example. Based on the personal brands that Tom Hanks and Denzel Washington have established, it is very unlikely that either of them would get a call from some weird, unestablished movie producer. Their brands say, "Hell, no! Don't even think about it." The same is true for you. When your brand identity is done right, the cheap, lemme-get-the-hookup, can-you-pour-it-in-my-hand-for-a-dime clients won't bother to waste your time.

Anyone who is not ready to make a serious investment in your services should be able to look at how you do it and decide, right away, that this is not the place for them.

Let's look at each element of your brand identity:

Brand Colors

Start with your brand colors. Ideally, you want to choose between two to three brand colors and definitely no more than six. The colors should complement each other (don't pair a hot orange with a dirty, muted brown) so if your brand is bubbly and bright, choose your colors accordingly.

You want to give deeper consideration to your colors beyond what your personal favorites are or what colors appeal to you. Your brand colors have a psychological component to them, so you should know the psychology of the colors that you're using. What do you want to express? Are you seeking to attract men or women? Is your audience older or younger?

Since these colors will represent your personal brand, it's also a great exercise to ask people who actually know you to describe you in words. I actually did this when I set out to choose colors for my own brand, and it completely turned me in a different direction. I'd originally planned to use red and black (my favorite colors), but the feedback I got about my personality included words like colorful, fun, full of life, cool, bright, and passionate. So I decided to use the brightest colors on the planet that spoke to my personality in the way that other people perceived me. It was one of the best decisions that I made.

Your colors should be a blend of who you are and who you want as a client.

If you are undecided about which colors may complement each other, try Pinterest. Search for wedding décor in the colors you are considering, and see what comes up. That will give you a visual of how those colors look together.

Brand Patterns

When you think about brands like Louis Vuitton and Gucci, you immediately think of their distinct brand pattern. A pattern is not required, but it does reinforce brand recognition and gives your brand dimension. Another benefit of using a pattern is that you can use it as a background for graphics. For example, instead of using stock photography for your social media quote images, you can customize your graphics with your brand pattern as the background, add a quote, and BOOM.

Logo

I could beat around the bush with this, but I won't:

Microsoft ClipArt has no place in your branding. *At all.*

I highly recommend working with a professional graphic designer for all of your visual branding, but if budget is a concern, the logo is the one thing you don't want to skimp on or attempt to do yourself. As you are sourcing the right professional designer to create a logo for you, keep in mind what actually makes a logo amazing:

Diverse, but not overcomplicated

A good logo is creative but simple. You don't want a logo that is extremely graphics heavy and hard for people to read. This isn't the time to make the letter C into something that looks like a W. Don't get so fancy that no one knows what in the hell your logo says.

Easy to Recognize

Your logo should be easy to spot.

A great logo should be designed so that it can be used in numerous ways, including billboards, car decals, t-shirts, and something as simple as your letterhead. You're going big, so be ready for it.

Designed in Adobe Illustrator

There is a distinct difference between a logo designed in Adobe Illustrator and ones that are designed in programs like Photoshop or Canva. Logos designed in Illustrator are vector based, so you can scale them to any size without losing the quality.

Typography

Typography is a fancy word for the fonts you'll use in your visual branding. What may look like some letters that are just thrown together on some of your favorite brand identities like Apple and Chipotle are actually well-thought-out elements. The most commonly used font styles are:

- Serif

- Sans Serif

- Script

When choosing your fonts, you should use a combination of two out of the three. Select styles that complement each other, for example, a serif and a sans serif, or a script and a sans serif. You should also use separate fonts for titles, subtitles, and body copy.

For the mother of sweet baby Jesus, please do not use an excessive number of fonts. Too many styles crowd your artwork and make it difficult for anyone who is reading your content to focus. Have you noticed that books are all in one sans serif font and not in script? That's because they should be easy to read. You want people to consume your content easily and read it well.

While we're on the topic of what not to do when it comes to fonts, here are a few more suggestions:

- Limit your font styles to no more than three.

- Avoid using scripts over a busy color or pattern.

Do a little research on typography to gain a better understanding of how words should flow in a certain design aesthetic. You can also flip through a few magazines to get a feel for how fonts can be used in your own work. Movie covers, book covers, CD and DVD covers are also great examples to study.

Once you decided which fonts you'd like to use, I recommend purchasing them to ensure you have the proper licensing to use them. As an alternative, there are plenty of free font websites, but be sure to look for sites that have free-use licenses and royalty-free options.

Branding Style Guide

Once you've defined your visual branding, creating a branding style guide is how to stay consistent with it. It should include your colors, fonts, brand patterns, and style of photography that you use, including stock photography.

Remember, visuals don't just stop at your website. Your brand identity should be congruent across all of your platforms, so your social media headers and graphics, for example, should use the same visual elements as your website.

A SITE (THAT IS NOT) FOR SORE EYES

Your website is your hub, your home, where people who are interested in you can find out more. Whenever you launch a new marketing campaign, you'll have to create a new landing page and new marketing material, but your personal brand website is the place where all your projects are connected. Think of it as your resume—it is a somewhat quick glance at who you are, what your business is about, and what value you can bring to potential customers.

If you sell yourself right, you're hired.

Social media is great and necessary, but your Facebook and Instagram pages cannot be the extent of your online presence.

I repeat, social media cannot be the extent of your online presence.

Your social media pages live on someone else's platform, so that means the images and words that you've posted there belong to the company, not you. Facebook owns your business page and your Instagram feed. If they were to be wiped out, all of your content goes with them.

Own your domain name. Own your infrastructure. Own your website. Period.

You want to build a site that is personable, professional, and by all means profitable. Consider these essentials of a great website as you set out to create your own:

A great website should be goal oriented. Why is someone coming here and what do you want them to do once they arrive? For example, if you are setting out this week to close deals with 100 new clients, is your website set up and optimized to attract those clients? Whatever your goal is, the first thing anyone sees when they come to your site is something that drives them to take that specific action.

A great website should invite people to experience you. This, friends, is what an opt-in is all about. An opt-in is that freebie or a little bitty piece of content that proves that you know what you're talking about. Ideas include a video training, audio training, interviews, tools and resource guides (get creative).

A great website should be frequently updated. You want a secure website that you can change on an as-needed basis. You should update your website's backend and content at least once a month.

Choosing the Right Platform

When it comes to designing your website, there are a number of platforms to consider. Some are better suited to DIY design, while others are bit more complicated, particularly from a coding perspective, and are best in the hands of a professional designer. I prefer to use Squarespace and Adobe Muse. As a designer, Adobe Muse is currently my favorite website platform, and what I love the most about the software, is the ability to customize websites. While other platforms use templates to make design easier, the downside is that all of the websites on a particular platform can start to look alike, and also restrict you in terms of the functions and features you may want or need.

I've built several websites using Adobe Muse, and they all look completely different. Adobe Muse's security is also top-notch, which means the likelihood of spam, excessive pop-ups, or crashing is minimal. These are all things you want to consider when choosing your platform. A professional designer can help you to navigate your options and choose the right platform for you.

DIY

If you are planning to design your own website, here are a few things that you'll need to familiarize yourself with, and some essential questions to answer as you set out to put on your graphic designer's hat and get started:

Wireframing: Wireframing is used to design layout and user experience and to help users to effectively flow through your website. The layout of your site, including any buttons or menus, is all wireframed. So you want to consider your user experience and how to build a site that optimizes that experience for them.

Content Flow: Considering how you want your content to flow is important. How many pages will the site have? What types of assets, like video clips, audio clips, images, and copy will you need on each page? Is the site mobile responsive and SEO optimized?

Call to Action: You also want to be clear on what the call to action is. What do you want people to do when they come to your site?

Getting Started

If you are not ready to go full-out with a professionally designed, customized website, there are some easy options to help you to get started with a basic site. Leadpages is a great alternative. You can choose a pre-designed landing page, plug in your content, and go live. The software is easy to use and the templates are extremely affordable. You could easily be up and running with a site that looks professional and sleek for as little as $50.

Another advantage to Leadpages is that you can refresh your website on demand, so you don't necessarily have to hire a designer to keep your site updated. If you decide to add a page, you can design the page yourself and relaunch your new and improved site.

Leadpages also does an exceptional job with software updates, so you'll always have the latest, hottest technology you need to grow your business.

<u>Going Pro</u>

The cost of hiring a professional designer to create a website for you can range anywhere from $1,500 to $10,000.

The cost of the relief from the headaches, sweat, and tears that come with trying to do-it-yourself? Priceless.

Sometimes you just have to let it go.

As a professional designer, there are a lot of things that I can do in my business. I can build my own site, design my own graphics, essentially anything that is related to the visual side of my agency, I can do. But there are other things that are just not my lane. So if it's not branding and marketing related, chances are I am hiring someone else to do it. Could I write my own sales copy? Probably and I actually did when I first launched my company. But now, I would rather pay an amazing copywriter to do it while I focus on the aspects of my business that I excel in and require me to personally handle.

As an up-and-coming CEO, you have to begin to make the decisions that are in the best interest of you, your sanity, and your company. Take my advice and let pros do what pros do. Figure out where you need to invest and where you can pick up the slack. And always keep in mind that time is money, baby.

When you are searching for the right designer, here is a list of questions to ask:

- What kind of design software do you use?

- What is your design process?

- What are your weaknesses?

- Do you have a portfolio that I can view?

- What's your website URL?

- How long have you been a designer?

- What are the deliverables that I will receive?

- What's the time frame for this project?

- How many revisions are included in this project?

- What kind of rights will I have to this design?

- How do your payments work?

- How do I get started with you?

- How will we communicate during my project? (Phone, email, or a combination of both?)

GET YOUR PRO PHOTO ON

Branded images are a must for your personal brand identity. While an occasional selfie or candid photo is great, you want professional, branded images for your website, marketing material, and packaging. If your face is on the cover of anything, it should be a pro photo.

By now, you've probably seen my face somewhere in your world. (Yup, that's me on the cover of this book.) The images that I use everywhere are branded. You'll notice everything about the photos, down to the colors of my skirt, aligns with my brand. That is not an accident, and you should give the same attention to detail.

You want photos that express your personality, and along with the rest of your brand identity, they should convey your worth. In other words, they should look expensive. If people see some cheap, unprofessional photo of you front and center on your website, they will automatically draw the conclusion that you are—you guessed it—cheap and janky. Don't allow some selfie in your bathroom mirror be the face of your brand. Invest in a professional photo shoot. Find a professional photographer who gets branding, gets you, and doesn't necessarily have a one-size-fits-all approach to photography. You want to work with someone who is dynamic enough to capture your brand in the way that you want to portray it.

When you are hiring a professional photographer, here is a list of questions to ask her:

- What kind of editing software do you use?

- What is your photo shoot process?

- What kind of photography are you great at?

- Do you have a portfolio that I can view?

- What's your website?

- How long have you been a photographer?

- How many photos will I receive?

- Will I own the copyrights to my photos that I take with you?

- If I would like more photos, how much will it cost?

- How many looks may I have?

- Do you have a studio or will the shoot be on-location?

- Do you know of any good MUA's (Makeup Artists?)

- If I hire a team to help me, do I need to purchase more studio time?

- How do I get started and how do your payment terms work?

A PSA About Your Look:

How you look matters, people. The clothes that you wear, your hair, your makeup—all of those things are important when it comes to your branding and how you show up, both on and offline. Audiences associate you with what you wear and how you look. It becomes a signature.

You expect Oprah to be classy.

You expect to see Beyoncé in sky-high heels.

You expect to see Janelle Monáe in black and white, at least in her early industry days.

You expect to see Erykah Badu in Afrocentric clothing, head wraps, and really funky jewelry pieces.

So for speaking engagements, videos—anywhere you show

up on a camera or in front of people—be aware and be on brand.

Stepping off the soapbox.

Personal Brand Jumpstart Steps

- Lead with your name

- Purchase your domain (YourName.com)

- Take at least one personality-based assessment

- Have your brand identity, logo, and personal brand website professionally designed

- Get a well-branded photo shoot done

- Set up your personal brand social media platforms

CHAPTER FIVE
HOW TO JUMPSTART YOUR SPEAKING PLATFORM

It may sound simple, but you speak so that people can hear you.

As you are building your personal brand, speaking offers you the opportunity to insert your perspective, your ideas, and your approach to the conversations that are buzzing in your industry. If you don't like it, you have an opportunity to say it.

And in fact, you should.

Think about our last presidential campaign. You had two candidates in the end, both of whom were complete opposites. Each held a position on a particular issue, and in some cases, one played it safer and more buttoned-up than the other. One guy wasn't afraid to speak his mind, to go against the grain, or to say what may have been considered unpopular, or even radical. While his opponent tried to please everybody by attempting to play it safe, dude spoke his truth and appealed to those who believed him. We all know what the outcome was—he won. And, might I add, stayed true to his personal brand for the entire election. Like it or love it, he was clear about how he showed up and people responded favorably to it.

My point is to speak your truth and allow those who rock with your message and your perspective choose to connect with you and to you.

Speaking doesn't just happen on a stage. When you hop on social media—YouTube, Periscope, or Facebook Live—and share your point of view, that's speaking too. You don't have to rant all of the time either. You could be teaching content or sharing a positive take on something in your industry. Wherever you choose to speak, use it as a platform and a place for you to be able to do so.

Speaking gives power to your perspective. Don't be afraid of your own voice.

When I decided to publish my own magazine, I began to host a lot of live events. Although nobody was more passionate about my work than I was, I hired an emcee for all of them, telling myself that it made sense to turn that over to someone who loved the stage while I focused on the behind the scenes stuff. The truth was, I was terrified. It wasn't until I made the shift to marketing and branding that I decided to throw my middle finger to the wind and just get out there. I knew I had to be the person who got on stage to share my point of view on the things that I was teaching. Nobody else could do that for me.

Now, I said I shook off my fear a little bit. But I didn't say I killed it right out of the gate. In fact, I sucked. Big time.

If you were to listen to my content, it would be painfully obvious that I really wasn't good at speaking or articulating my ideas. But I kept going. I eventually put together my very first video training, 10 Steps to Launching a Premium Brand. Perfect, right? I thought so too. I know I am a beast at design so my slides would be amazing, and they were. As I was pulling the content together, I was taking screen grabs, posting pictures on Instagram. The more I prepared, the better I felt about the visuals. Now I just had to figure out how to talk about all of the great content on these slides without sounding like an idiot. So I decided to write a script.

I must have recorded that video 10, 15, 20 times. Even with the script, I kept repeating stuff, fumbling over my words, and I couldn't figure out how to edit the parts that I messed up, so I would have to record the entire thing again every time. That didn't matter to me because I was determined to make it perfect. I recorded and rerecorded until I nailed it. The final cut wasn't perfect, but I was still proud of it. I finally released the video and it actually was a hit. I made a lot of dough from it. I was totally poppin' my collar.

Until I got an inbox message.

"I like your video, [insert a big-assed BUT here] but it sounded like you were reading. Were you reading? I can tell. Let me give you a tip, next time you record you should have bullet points and you shouldn't read them from the paper."

Really?

Here I was celebrating my first big launch and counting money that I never had from that whack-ass video (yes, I can be honest about it, I just didn't need her to be) and I was getting criticized. I was a little discouraged, but if I was real with myself, I knew she was right. The only way for me to get better was to try again. I decided to jump right into my next attempt, a three-part video series. But before I could get that recorded and released, the unthinkable happened. I was invited to speak at a well-known women's conference.

I agonized over that stage for months. The day finally came and I was shaking in my shoes for the entire ride. All of my fears came up—I'd been avoiding stages until I felt more pre- pared and like more of an expert. I didn't know if I was ready for this, but I'd already said yes, and I wasn't backing out.

I am not sure what happened on that stage, but anyone watching would have thought I'd been professionally speak- ing for thirty years. I'd created this phenomenal presenta- tion, rehearsed each and every line a thousand times, yet I didn't talk about half of it. Something took over me, and I just started speaking from what I felt. I fed on the energy of the audience and, to be honest, I just didn't want to fail. I knew that I had the knowledge and the expertise—I just needed to let it flow. And it did.

From that experience, I went on to speak more and more often, presenting and teaching on my own platforms and others'. As my brand grew and became more visible, I started getting more calls for interviews. I couldn't risk sounding like an idiot, so I had no choice but to master speaking. I went from shaking in my shoes to standing tall in my voice.

I hope that chick that threw shade in my inbox has seen your girl lately. (I had to get that dig in.)

There are a number of reasons why we're afraid to get out there and speak. Some of it is fear from our own experiences and hang-ups, while some of it we absorb from other people's stuff. How many times have you watched someone flop on television and vowed that will never be you? So instead of getting out there and at least trying, you hide.

Speaking is probably the most important thing that you will ever do because it gives voice to your thoughts. And believe me, the last thing that you want is to fire up your social media one day and hear some rookie spitting out the point of view that's been stuck in your head because you were too afraid to share it. Don't let that happen to you.

Speaking is like poppin' wheelies on your first big girl bike. You'll never hit them until you hop on and learn to ride.

Now get on off that sidewalk.

CONFIDENCE FOLLOWS FEAR

Here's a tidbit of advice for you—start small. Podcasting is a great way to ease into speaking, conquer your fear, and build your confidence. Another idea is to record some voice memos on your smartphone and share them with two people that you trust. If you'd prefer to give it a shot from in front of the camera, try Periscope. I actually committed to doing 100 Periscope broadcasts over a period of a few months, and each time, my confidence got better.

Once you've mastered one of those smaller efforts, upgrade a bit. Do a teleclass and invite 50-60 people to attend. Be ballsy enough to ask for some feedback or just wait for it. (Trust me, people have no problem sharing.) You'll find out everything that you need to know with a little patience. If your audience likes what you have to say, they'll rush to your website for more, they'll inbox you, Tweet you, and tell everybody in a Facebook post. If they think you suck, you will hear crickets. Pretty simple. But don't not get back on the bike. Try again, and keep pushing yourself to get in front of bigger and bigger audiences.

You don't always have to jump out into an ocean at first. Take your time and ease into it.

The true key to mastering your speaking ability and beating that fear down is simple—create your own content. When you are sharing your own ideas, information, and inspiration, you'll feel like talking is the most natural thing in the world. In fact, you can't speak if you don't know what you're talking about. Have you ever asked someone a question, and they're stuttering, pacing, eyes wandering? Dead giveaway that there is an amateur in your midst. People will peep you out as a fraud from a mile away. They can sniff out when you don't know what you're talking about, when you're scared, or you haven't done your research.

When you step out there, be prepared. Overly prepared.

What sucks more than flopping, or someone else stealing your ideas before you can give voice to them? Somebody else in the room outshining you on your own platform. We've all seen it happen before and it occurs because someone was overconfident and underprepared. Speaking doesn't always have to be stats and facts; it could be your opinion, your beliefs. When you are speaking on what you believe, you can't fake it.

And if given the chance, the words will just flow out of you.

Speaking is all about your point of view and fully understanding what you want to share, communicate, and simply talk to people about. TED Talks have proven that speaking doesn't have to be stuffy or highly structured, even when you are teaching something educational. The best talks are delivered from a place of belief, and strong perspectives and ideas around a particular topic.

Fear less and speak more.

DEVELOPING YOUR OWN POINT OF VIEW

When you are new to speaking, you want to be anything but generic. Audiences are seeking fresh perspectives and new ideas. You want to hear, "Wow, that's new," as opposed to "Haven't I heard this somewhere before?" People want innovation and integration.

Integration means to take a concept, a theory, or best practice that you may be using in one industry and apply it to another. Can you diversify your content? For example, if you're a makeup artist and you're asked to speak at an automotive conference, can you take something from your business, perhaps a signature system for booking new clients, and apply it? Let's say you're a social media guru, and you have a signature talk entitled, "15 Ways to Use Social Media." How would you apply that to a church or the beauty industry? That requires you to do a little digging to understand your concepts and to research that industry to figure out how to translate those ideas. Once you do, you may change that presentation title to something like, "7 Advanced Strategies Beauty Professionals Need to Grow Their Social Media Following." Your new topic is more specific and now it sounds exclusive to beauty pros. Who wouldn't jump on that?

Innovation comes into play when you are bringing your own ideas to the forefront. What can you talk about in your industry that no one else can? Those who are early adopters will always thrive because they are the first to take heed to what's new. Strive to stay in that group.

Stop being a reporter and start becoming an insider.

And speaking of reporting, don't disregard what's happening in the news and in current events. Use what's happening to join a trending conversation and make it relevant to your business. Topics that are in the news are a great opportunity to bring your personal story into the conversation. Connect the two and share your personal point of view while speaking from experience.

Before you begin to seek out other platforms, be sure that you can comfortably convey your own ideas and concepts to your own audience. You need to have some followers, some people who agree with your perspectives and your philosophy, even if it's a small group of people.

WHERE DO YOU WANT TO BE SEEN?

Creating your own platform is as simple as hosting your own online event. The online world offers numerous places for you to speak. Some options are:

- Webinars

- Telecasts and Classes (your own or someone else's)

- Periscopes

- Facebook Live

- Instagram Live

- Broadcasting

- YouTube Videos

On any platform, show up well. If you're on video, make sure your clothes are on point. If it's just audio, check your tone, your introduction, and even the words that you use. Those words are branded language, and ideally, you want to craft your own and use it as much as possible. Your language is part of your brand identity too. Think about what kind of brand language you can create and use it consistently for every conversation that you have regarding your business.

I have a couple of additional tips for you as you're planning your first online event:

- Speak your ass off, whether one person or 1,000 people attend your event. You never know who is in your audience and you want to get into the habit of showing up exceptional.

- If you are not making a sales offer at the end of your online event, you should at least offer something of value to attendees at no cost. Leverage events to build your email list; you don't always have to have something to sell.

FEE OR FREE?

When it comes time for you to explore offline speaking engagements, the question of money is bound to come up. You may be new to speaking, but you are an expert. So you feel torn between going for the money and chalking it up to experience. The real answer is you need both.

Free opportunities offer experience. Paid opportunities offer expertise.

Non-paid speaking engagements definitely add value to your bottom line. You have a chance to not only learn something and strengthen your skills, but you also connect with new people, build relationships, and leverage your other audiences.

When you are paid to speak, it signifies that you are a true expert. Getting paid enhances your credibility—once you're offered a check, more than likely, those opportunities will keep coming.

If you get a call with an offer to set foot on a stage, virtually or physically, you always need to assess if this is the right thing for you:

<u>Know Thy Host</u>

Find out what you can about the host, including their previous events and their audience. You want to determine if their target market and brand aligns with yours. You should also look into (or ask) the cost of the event. This will tell you a lot about what type of event you can expect, and if there will be real opportunities for you to generate leads or sales. Keep in mind that most free events draw "free-minded" people—when someone pays to attend a conference or a seminar, that's a sign that they are open to investing.

Who Else Is In the Room?

In addition to attendees, you also want to look at what other industry peeps are speaking or presenting. Are they game-changers? Do they have strong brands and a respectable following? Sponsorships, or lack thereof, are also telling. If a host can draw major corporate sponsorships, that's a big deal.

JUST DO IT

I know it sounds cliché, ya'll, but for real, you gotta just jump out there. I've given you some ideas on how to get started, and now it's time to do it.

Speaking Jumpstart Start Tips

- Develop your point of view

- Build an audience

- Host your own event or get on someone else's platform

- Do it repeatedly until you build your confidence

CHAPTER SIX
THE POWER OF PUBLISHING

By now it's probably clear that I believe in owning your stuff. We've talked about owning your name. We've discussed owning your voice and your perspective. We've covered owning your platform. Now, as we build that platform, we have to talk about printing on it.

So let's chat about publishing.

I know you are reading this book because you want a business that makes money. And you know that I believe that you absolutely should. But these businesses—these brands—that we're building are also about your legacy. Not that publishing won't put a few duckets (actually, hopefully, a lot of them) in your pocket, but it will also give you so much more.

Publishing lives on without you. We can all think of books—*Who Moved My Cheese*, *Raving Fans*, *The E-Myth*—that have been around for decades that still have influence and impact and are still selling thousands, if not millions, of copies every year. Through books, you can speak to generations beyond your own. There are children who were born yesterday, coming into the world as you're flipping these pages, who will read what you create in print. Just think, there will be some know-it-all college student who could be holding your book in his hands twenty years from now. It could be your book that sets a new standard for how we live life. It could be your book that drives some significant change in our culture. It could be your book that sits at the top of the New York Times Bestseller List.

But you have to write it first.

Real Talk Moment:

Writing a book is probably one of the scariest—no, 'eff that—
the scariest thing that I've ever done. It was the one thing
I hadn't checked off of my professional bucket list. Every
expert that I admired and looked up to had published a book
(several, in fact) so I knew it was something I had to do. It
wasn't just an option for me to get it done, at all, but I was
still avoiding it like a seventh-grade geometry test.

The crazy thing was that my confidence is on a thousand,
hell, one hundred thousand, when it comes to what I know
and what I do, but there was something about putting it in
print that terrified me. With everything that I had done, all of
the training, teaching, traveling the country (and the world
through my content), I was still shaky about the process. I
had enough knowledge and experience in me for ten books,
but I didn't feel like I had enough to say. So I was prepared
to keep running from it and telling myself that I'd eventually
get around to it when in actuality I probably would have just
continued to re-negotiate the "I'm gonna do this!" date with
myself.

But then it hit me.

I was a straight-up hypocrite.

Here I was, coaching clients left and right on the power of

publishing, especially books, and how necessary it was to their personal brands, profits, and careers. Yet I hadn't done it myself. Sure, I had published other content, but I had been ducking and dodging that book thing for *years*. I decided I couldn't hide from it—or myself—anymore. I had to stop being a punk and start practicing what I preached.

And now here we are. You are not just holding a book in your hands. You are holding the result of me finally facing my biggest fear. You are holding something I'd dreamed about. You are holding a part of my legacy. Long after I am gone, this book will still be here—teaching, telling, and changing the way that people do business.

Writing and publishing your own content, like books, is the only way to keep your voice alive in this world.

So I want you to think about what you want to leave in this world. I want you to think about your legacy. And while you're at it, I want you to think about my top reasons (I could go on and on) for writing and publishing your own book:

Books open doors. Books take you places, baby. When you write a book, it automatically says you are credible and that you know your stuff. As a result, people want to know you, hear you, and ultimately pay you. A book can literally take you from a nobody to a somebody overnight, and honestly, there is no other form of media that can do that. Even if your brand is already crushing it in the universe, a book only elevates that status to stratosphere level. Can you imagine what will happen when Beyoncé and Kanye West decide to release their first books?

Most experts that you see with regular features on news and television programs are authors. Patrice Washington, author of the *Real Money Answers* series, is a prime example of leveraging a book to build a brand and a platform. You've probably seen her on the *Steve Harvey Show*, CNN, Bloomberg News—everywhere. These major news outlets are willing to offer their stages and their audiences to her because she is so legit.

Books demand respect. Everybody knows that writing a book ain't easy. We know that creating a book is a lengthy process. It's hard. It takes time. It takes money. It takes a boldness (also known as balls) to put what you know in a book for other people to see. When people see your name on the cover of a book, they sit up and take notice. I personally wanted the challenge of writing a book because I knew that regardless of how much I had to invest, the reward I would reap would be so much greater. I had published workbooks and other content, but I knew I could not stop there. Books are the epitome of expertise.

Books are also about credibility. Not only will clients see you more as an expert when you've published a book, but so will the industry. As a speaker, when you apply to larger organizations to speak at a conference or an event, one of the most common questions is "have you written a book?" Authorship is a discriminator. It says that you are a pro and you've reached that expert status. Frankly, there was no way that I could call myself a legit expert and not have published a book. The same is true for you.

And people still read books. I know that all of the content that we find online makes you think that books are irrelevant, but that is so not true. People still read books and, in fact, we *need* books to learn from.

NO TIME LIKE THE PRESENT

There is no better time to become an author than right now. The independent publishing world is wide open, unlike the world we lived in a decade or two ago.

I decided to go the independent route, but I was committed to a first-class process. I wanted to go legit. So I ran a full-out campaign with all of the bells and whistles—launch team, publicist, and book launch—the whole nine. It was so important for me to do this right. Going for it as an independent author doesn't mean you have to cut any corners. You can still show up big without a big publisher behind you.

Let me share a few more things for you to consider when publishing your book:

Self-Publishing vs. Traditional Publishing:

As an author, you have two options, to go for it and do it all on your own, or to work with a publishing house. When you self-publish, you take on the role of the publisher, meaning that you not only write your book, but you handle the design, the printing, the marketing—all of it—independently. When you opt to go with a publisher, you start with a book proposal, shop it to see who picks it up, and after they do, they handle all of the development and everything else for you. So there are advantages to both.

I decided to go the independent route primarily because I wanted to run my own ship (I know, you're surprised, right?). I wanted full creative control over the development, marketing, and even the sale of my book. Most traditional publishing houses have a signature framework that all of their authors follow, and I knew I didn't want to be like everybody else. Think about how tight you'd like to hold the reins of your own book creation process. Independent may be the right route for you too.

On-Demand Printing and Mass Printing: The days of riding around with a trunk full of books are kinda over. CreateSpace and Ingram Sparks are both options to make the sales and printing part of publishing so much easier with the ability to print on demand.

Printed and Digital Formats: You can—and should—publish

your book in multiple formats. In addition to print books, consider digital formats, like Kindle, as well as audiobooks, which you can sell through Audible.

GET SOMETHING PUBLISHED

Besides being just a little bit afraid, another reason why I opted to publish at this point in my career as opposed to before is that I wanted to be sure that I'd built a solid platform *first*. If I am being honest with myself, I wasn't one-hundred percent ready to write a book a few years ago. I needed a powerful personal brand (check) and I needed to have made some phenomenal strides in the speaking realm (double check). It's not a coincidence that publishing is the third phase of my *Seven Phases* framework —it takes some elbow grease to get ready.

You may be in the process of developing your brand and platform before you jump out there and publish your first book, and that's cool. But that doesn't mean you shouldn't publish anything. When it comes to publishing, there are a number of mediums that you can leverage with your personal brand:

- Books

- Workbooks

- Journals

- Guides

- Reports

- Articles

- Columns

- Magazines

- Blogs

- Vlogs

One of the aspects that I love most about publishing is that you make it happen yourself. Content is an opportunity to showcase you, your expertise, and your work. I created a magazine because nobody really gave a damn about up-and-coming artists like me. I wasn't going to wait until somebody valued my work enough to give it some shine. I constructed my own stage and flooded it with a spotlight—not just for me, but for other artists to thrive, celebrate themselves, and to keep each other inspired as we continued to do our work in the world.

That's the thing about creating and owning something. You get to bring others right along with you.

DO MORE THAN THE NORM

Beyond just positioning you as an expert, your published content should keep your audience interested, so you have to—you guessed it—actually be interesting. You don't have to do the same boring stuff that everyone else is doing. Fire up their engagement with some fresh content:

Product Demos and Reviews: If you're excited about a new product, share it with viewers. Audiences appreciate it when someone other than companies brags about how awesome a product is.

Company and Industry News: What's going on in your industry? Inquiring client and customer minds want to know too, so don't keep it to yourself or save those conversations for your peer groups. The same thing goes for your company news—tell people what you're up to, what you're creating. Facebook, for example, does a really good job of telling users what's new within the company, like product updates. They have a blog and regularly share information in a cool, social way.

Behind the Brand Content: People really like to know what's going on behind the scenes. If you're in the process of creating a new product, share your development before the launch. It may not all be pretty, but audiences don't mind. Bloopers and outtakes are just as interesting as the main show.

Trending Topics: I mentioned this as a way to develop your point of view and unique perspective, so do the same thing for your business. What's happening in the world right now that you can tie to your business or your specific services? Stay on top of what's trending on Facebook, Twitter, and Instagram. Get in on the conversations that your followers are talking about. Don't just offer your personal opinion and leave it at that. Link your point of view back to your expertise.

Research and Insights: Being an insider requires that you know and share information before the masses have access to it. Become known as an early adopter so that people begin to look to you first for what's hot. Share insightful and fresh content as opposed to always responding to what's already out there.

Repurposed Content: Can you turn your e-book into an audio book? How about a movie or a short film? Think about how you can leverage your content in more than one format.

Fun Stuff: I recently started sharing some fun, animated .gifs and my audience loves them! Think about some ways to get creative too. Instead of creating t-shirts, try an old-school style movie poster. Introduce your company with a full-fledged course and give it away as an opt-in. Get people talking about you!

GET EXCLUSIVE

Publishing private license content is intellectual property that you create and distribute through a mutual contract with an organization or a bigger company. The content can only be purchased through that company, who in turn pays you for exclusive rights.

Let's say you are a personal finance expert and you decide to write a budget guide for college students to teach them about managing money responsibly and reducing debt. Instead of pushing that book through Amazon, you could sell the rights to a bookstore for a large college or university or, better yet, a textbook publisher for national distribution.

Your popular signature systems, programs, and products can also be taken off the market by other companies, allowing you to make money off the grid. Explore exclusive publishing opportunities by identifying companies who are ideal distribution channels for your content and establishing relationships with them. Also keep in mind that these partnerships don't have to last a lifetime. You could enter into an exclusive rights agreement for five years, leverage the opportunity, and then at the end of the contract, put your stuff back out into the mainstream.

Publishing Quick Start Tips

- Decide when you are going to publish your first book.

- Consider some other content that you can publish besides a book.

- Start writing and publish your content.

CHAPTER SEVEN
ATTENTION GRABBING MEDIA

When a powerful personal brand is running on all cylinders, mass media is definitely fuel for the engine. Be it television, radio, print, or podcast, media is the spotlight that shines brightly on your brilliance. There's the type of media with an open-door policy that enables you to drive the hype with your own content (think social media) and then there is traditional media, like television or radio, which operate more on an invitation-only basis.

Your next yes could present itself on either platform. So get ready.

Good or bad, media is the center of our universe. Whether we're tuned into our Facebook feed, CNN, or TMZ, we look to media for insight into what's going on in our world and to keep us constantly dialed into what's happening around us. But beyond news, we look to media outlets that we trust for recommendations on products and people alike. How many times have you heard about a new book or blender on your favorite talk show and ran (not walked) to your laptop to order one for next day delivery?

Media heavily influences our perception of what's hot, and likewise, what sucks.

Guess what side of the conversation you want to fall on?

PEOPLE ARE GONNA TALK, SO IT MAY AS WELL BE

ABOUT YOU, BOO

Since we know that media controls what the world is discussing moment by moment, the key is to get your brand among today's hottest topics. You know like I know that your brand and your brilliance are much more important than the latest celebrity divorce or somebody's recent set of booty implants. (I mean, we all like a little tea, but the world needs substance too.) People need something to discuss—always. So let it be you.

Here's why media is so important to your personal brand and why you need folks buzzing about you:

Exposure to new audiences. As your brand expands and your visibility increases, so should your audiences. Media gets you in front of not only more people, but more diverse fans and potential clients. Your next million dollar customer could be flicking through channels this morning or flipping through a magazine, waiting for your high-wattage smile to pop up. I recently had a celebrity show up on one of my live broadcasts to check me out and she even reached out to me afterward in Facebook Messenger to chat it up. Dope, right? If I'd just limited my reach to one form of media, we probably would never have connected. Show up wherever you can.

Bring awareness to your expertise. Media offers you multiple platforms to tell people what you know and to show them what you do. You can sell new products or tell the world about a new service. Your media appearances are opportunities to turn audiences into fans and fans into clients. And media is not just for sales. Maybe you want to shine a light on a special cause that you genuinely support or a non-profit partnership. Media can help do that while positioning you as an advocate for an effort or organization.

Create social value. When people see you frequently and begin to associate you with something, your name starts to accumulate social value. In their minds, you start to become known for this or that, and, eventually, your name will become synonymous with it. Media is a vehicle to make it happen.

MEDIA CAN TAKE YOU BUT THEY CAN'T MAKE YOU

One of the common misconceptions about media is that it makes you legit in the world.

We've even talked about some examples throughout this book where someone's viral video went bananas, and now everybody is talking about it and them. So I know it seems that these people became overnight sensations, as a result of a few well-timed media appearances. And in some respects, that's true. *For them.* But how does it work in the real world? The business world?

The media is not looking for anyone to put on. They are looking for people who are already on.

Most media outlets seek out guests or interesting (emphasis on interesting) folks to feature based on their personalities, and not solely on their content. Talk show hosts know that Oprah will deliver a shitload of wisdom and those "a-ha" moments. Tyler Perry will almost always talk about his Christian-based beliefs and values, Steve Harvey will have something to say about risking it all to gain success, and Gary Vaynerchuk will cuss like a sailor. Show hosts or journalists are thinking first about how each personality will align with their audiences and the topic that they are seeking to share. The fact that any of them have books, movies, or other poppin' projects is secondary.

Your personality is what gets you in the door. Your content is what you leverage once you are inside.

This is why your personal brand is so important. You want a brand that stands out, delivers value, but also feels like a real person is connected to it. All of the people that I mentioned are perceived to be experts, but they are personalities too. They are well-known, well-liked (most of the time), and well-respected. Who wouldn't want somebody like that in their article or on their stage?

Is that somebody you?

When you do win the world over and get a chance to shine

bright like a diamond in the media, keep this golden rule in mind:

Media adds to your credibility. It can't make you credible.

The media, especially national platforms, tell people that you're so good that "these folks over here" are talking about you too. It's not just your Moms, a few friends, and local audiences that are raving about you, but you're so hot that major outlets want to feature you. Showing up on a nationally syndicated radio show or newspaper screams credibility. Most people know that not just anybody is gonna walk up into a news station and take a seat—no, there are levels to this. If you show up on somebody's flat screen in their living room, that means something major.

But you have to have something else to show for your life than a few media mentions.

To be honest, media shouldn't be on your radar until you've built an online presence for people to see.

YOUR MEDIA MIX

When people Google you, you don't want them to hear crickets. We live in a world where the more mentions there are of you, the more credible your brand appears. So, when It comes to media appearances, a little of this and a little of that is a good thing. You want a good blend of both social and traditional media so people can find and see you both on and offline.

An ad in the newspaper used to be enough—not so much anymore. That ad is great, but do you have a Facebook page and an Instagram account? Can I find a couple of videos on YouTube? Today's consumer expects to see you in all of the right places.

The most engaged, most relevant, most up-to-date person will always get the bank. Period.

So you have to been seen everywhere.

Let's talk about how.

Please, Please Get Social

We'll talk a lot about traditional media in this chapter, because I believe in it, wholeheartedly. But in today's digitally driven world, you must focus on social media. And dare I say that social media should be your main focus if you are launching a new brand. Word travels fast online and so you'll go further and faster by leveraging social media, at least initially.

Unlike traditional media, social media is always moving, changing, and evolving to stay current, while most print media, for example, hasn't changed in the last forty years. The way that you advertise in a newspaper hasn't changed, but

Facebook and Instagram have totally shifted how we market our businesses to segmented audiences. Social media challenges you to be better and not get comfortable.

I know—it can feel like too much to handle, but it's either grasp it or get left in the dust.

I talk to so many people who are still afraid of social media or who downright refuse to learn it. So they try, foolishly, to bury their head in the sand and ignore it. Not only is that an arrogant approach, but it's also a whack-ass reason not to get with the program. If you've been avoiding Facebook or Periscope because you think it's too hard, I need you to face your fears. The internet won't bite a hole in you, I promise. But not showing up on social media will put in a hole in your pocket. So let's get over the hump. Cool?

If you are just starting out on social media or you want to expand your engagement, choose the platforms that best suit your needs. When it comes to social media, you want to focus on legacy platforms or those with proven staying power. If the platform has been around for five or more years, chances are it will be here for a while. Facebook has added some new bells and whistles, but it's still here and pumping with no signs of slowing down. And there are other platforms for you to consider as well.

Let's look at each of the major players and I'll give you my two cents on each:

Periscope: I like Periscope because its audience is live, engaged, and hype. This platform gives you the type of engagement that you would typically spend hundreds of thousands of dollars on at no cost, with only one requirement—you have to stay consistent. Right now, Periscope is highly relationship-driven, and you'll meet some cool people on there.

Facebook: You can find the whole earth on Facebook. It's one of those platforms that's always evolving and it's becoming a little world all on its own. It's moving into livestreaming; add that to the ability to send money and make phone calls (yes, you can do all of that) and you will find that soon, you'll be able to access everything you need right from your Facebook account.

Facebook is really great for building long-lasting relationships and you can actually keep in touch with people as often as you'd like. There's the community aspect with Facebook groups, which encourages people who have common lifestyles, like moms, couples, and singles, to "hang out" together. Facebook gets how to target people, which is something that is extremely valuable to you as a business owner. The majority of my business comes from Facebook, so I love it.

YouTube: YouTube is always searchable, so if you want people to find you, especially from Google (Google actually owns YouTube) then you want your videos there. Even if you're a complete newbie, if you can get on YouTube and be the first one talking about something that is trending and hot, your video is guaranteed to get a lot of views. YouTube is a great way to get introduced to people who don't know you.

Twitter: Twitter gives you the opportunity to jump right into a conversation or news that is already happening, so it's timely and moves fast.

Instagram: Instagram (which is owned by Facebook) is really cool from a visual perspective. While the platform used to be limited to just sharing images, it's starting to evolve into so much more. Now there are business pages, messaging features, and real-time analytics and engagement which makes using hashtags off the chain! (Okay, I'll calm down. But y'all know I love this stuff!) Instagram Stories and Instagram Live are both new to the scene and are musts for engaging your audience. Keep an eye out for Instagram's shopping feature, a game-changer for anyone selling products online.

Oldies but Goodies

Traditional media may seem outdated, but it isn't at all. You still want to scoop "standard" media opportunities whenever you can. This includes:

Podcasts: National and global

Radio: Talk radio and commercial radio programs

TV: Local and national news, talk shows, commercials

Print: Magazines, newspapers (local, regional, national)

Since the doors of traditional media are a little more challenging to burst through, you may have to make your window. When I was new to the world of online marketing and
branding, I decided to create my own podcast for that very
reason—an opportunity didn't come my way fast enough,
so I made one. My podcast has been extremely successful,
reaching hundreds of thousands around the world.

That podcast was great for a number of reasons:

I created my own platform.

I got to control my own content which positioned me as an
expert.

I could speak on whatever topic I chose without worrying
about an interviewer's slant or filter.

I could distribute my content to other countries and leverage
mass distribution channels like iTunes, Stitcher, SoundCloud,
Google Play, iHeartRadio, and Apple TV.

As an expert, I am sure you have similar reasons why creating
your own platform makes sense. You may decide to start your
magazine or produce your own television show. Whatever
you decide to do, my point is that you don't wait until someone else deems you worthy of a shot at the mainstream me-

dia. The bigger opportunities will come, but in the meantime, in between time, do your own thing. There is a whole universe of people waiting to hear something that you have to say.

GIVE THE OFFLINE PEOPLE SOME LOVE TOO

I know it's a challenge to imagine a world before social media, but there really was one—and there still is. There is still a huge segment of the population (namely your Baby Boomers and even some Gen Xers) who don't live online the way that millennials do. More than likely, anyone who is over the age of 50 still prefers radio, newspaper, or some form of traditional media, so for them to find out about you, you need to show up where they are.

Keep in mind that not everyone who needs you will pop in on your Periscope or Facebook Live. But your offline audience is just as important as your online one. While your offline exposure and reach will move a little slower (in comparison to the fast fire of the internet), it's still extremely valuable.

So give those peeps some love too, and ensure that you stay fresh and relevant in all forms of media that make sense for your brand.

FREE MEDIA VERSUS PAID MEDIA

There is always a free and paid version of everything, and media is no exception. There are instances when people are asked to be on television, and then there are other scenarios when people pay. Talk show or news appearances are ideal examples of free media, while commercials count as paid media.

You may think that paid media is a better opportunity when, in fact, it's not. Anything paid is actually an interruption, and viewers are more likely to skip a paid segment than they are a free one. Think about if your favorite entrepreneur or celebrity shows up on *Good Morning America* one morning while you're rushing to get dressed for an appointment. You've been waiting around all morning to see her, and finally, the interview segment comes on and she's great. Now let's say that same person shows up on a commercial. Are you as inclined to miss your hair appointment to watch a commercial that provides no value to you (other than to sell you something) and may be on again a thousand times? Probably not. People pay to avoid interruptions, which is why Spotify and similar music streaming services are so popular.

You don't want your brand and your messaging wedged between shows. If you have a shot at media, you want to *be* the show. Or at least a part of it. So while commercials and ads are great when you can snag them, shoot for those segments or interviews to add into the mix.

And while we're on the topic of segments and television appearances, remember this: While one-off features and media appearances are great, the holy grail of media for an expert is a regular feature or segment on television or in print. Strive to be so good that they ask you back, again and again.

GETTING THE ATTENTION

Sometimes you have to beat your own drum and get the media to notice you. Once your brand is stellar and all of your ducks are in a row, the first step to landing those mainstream media mentions is to create a press kit. A solid press kit should include:

- A professional bio

- Branded, professional images

- A list of media appearances

- Your best case studies or testimonials

- Social media profiles, handles, and impressions

- Your current products and services

- Contact information

Your press kit is designed, printed, and ready to hit the streets. The ideal time to reach out to media is when you have something time-sensitive or relevant to a current event.

If your time is now, your first step is to pick the best media outlet for the audience that you want to reach (older audiences are more likely to be watching the local news than hanging out on Facebook). Next, craft a clear press release or pitch email to send out. You want to make it easy for the journalist or producer to find out exactly what you need. They are receiving thousands of pitches, so keep these tips in mind to make sure that yours stand out:

Include links to your website, photos, and any other relevant info

Check your website and make sure the links lead to information that is easy to navigate (consider a press page that has a .pdf version of your press kit, along with photos, media mentions, etc.)

Put everything you want to say in the body of the email and avoid attachments

Be clear about how your story will benefit the outlet; don't make people figure that out on their own. If the connection isn't obvious, you may get passed over.

Offer an exclusive if you have one. They key to exclusives is honesty. Give the journalist the first right to the story, but if you intend to shop around, say it. State in your pitch that if you don't receive a response within a certain amount of time, you will take the story to another outlet. It happens all the time, so don't be afraid, but do be straight up. It's not cool to have two outlets run an "exclusive" story at the same time. If that happens, you'll ruin any chance of a relationship with both.

You are selling yourself, so you have to write copy that grabs attention and sells.

DIY OR PRO

Let's have a quick chat about tackling this media mountain on your own or hiring a publicist to do some legwork for you. When you're doing you own PR, you have a lot to consider. First, you have to be on point with your writing, so you'll definitely need to put on your copywriter's hat. Tie the producer's ideas and segments for the show into your story and show how the two intersect. Second, you need to be creative enough to spin your story to fit multiple outlets and tailor your pitch to each. Blasting out a whack, cookie-cutter pitch is a sure-fire way to get your stuff thrown in the trash. Lastly, you need to know enough people in media to determine who is a good fit for you, your story, and your brand.

Enter the superhero publicist. Going pro for your publicity can save you tons of time and eventually money. In addition to being exceptional at crafting pitches, professional publicists have relationships and connections that they can leverage to get you in the door faster. There's no need for you to beat the streets (and your head against the wall) to find someone to give you the time of day when publicists have wined and dined enough reporters and producers to bypass the line and go straight to the VIP section. Consider investing in a professional, even if it's just once a year or during an important phase of your business, such as the release of your new book or a new product.

Can you pull it off on your own? Sure. You just need to be ready to put in the work.

FOR GOODNESS SAKES, BE READY

WHEN YOU GET THE CALL

True Story: My first television appearance was in 2010. At the time, a partner and I were co-producing an event, "Hearts and Arts," in Memphis, and somehow we landed an interview on the local news to drum up interest and ticket sales. Neither of us had been in front of a camera before—ever—and we were both scared shitless. As the anchorman started to fire off questions about the event and the inspiration behind it, we did a pretty good job of winging it. Until he turned to my partner and asked him about the non-profit that the proceeds from the event would be donated to.

Crickets

Dude totally froze and, for a few very uncomfortable seconds, we were both standing there looking like Tweedle Dee and Tweedle Dum. Fortunately, the interviewer spared our humiliated souls and quickly moved on. That leads me to my first point—

Know your shit. The last thing you want to is to be caught looking like a stunned deer in headlights when a news anchor asks you a question about something you should know like the back of your hand. If you're talking about your new product, know it inside out. If you're promoting an appearance at a local event, have the time, place, and even the co-hosts memorized. Now is not the time to wing it.

Wear your normal gear. There is no need to go grab Grandma's pearls (if you wouldn't ordinarily wear them) just because you're going on television. You want to be as comfortable as possible, so dress in your own clothes for the occasion. Borrowing grown-up clothes will only make you look awkward, so stay true to your style, whatever that is.

Use your real name. Unless you are a recording artist, there's no need to use a stage name. Remember, this is an opportunity to build your personal brand and you want to be able to leverage the appearance forever. Using your actual name keeps the media clip relevant and available to be referenced in your portfolio and media resume.

Get to know the network. You want to be as familiar as

possible with the program you'll be featured on. Familiarize yourself by watching a few older segments. Understand how the show normally flows and if there are any regular features so you don't get caught off guard. If you know all of Ellen's guests typically groove all the way to the couch, then you'll want practice your signature dance before the taping.

And on that note—

Get to know the on-air personalities. Research the talent or the personality who will likely interview you. You should be ready to draw them right into a discussion that is focused on you.

So if Whoopi asks me, "So Audria, tell me about your book?"

I may say something like, "Well, Whoopi, last year when you interviewed such and such, you mentioned that she likely missed that Oscar nod because she flopped during a major media appearance. That's exactly why I wrote, *Are You Ready for the Yes?*"

Always be ready to seize the moment. You have to keep in mind that a journalist's primary job is to spin a story to suit their audience. So being invited on a show is really just half the win—the other half is making sure that you actually get your point across. From the moment you step on set, you're competing against factors like commercial breaks, breaking news, and the next segment featuring a puppy in a tutu or a cooking demo. Be ready!

Media Jumpstart Tips

- Have something media worthy.

- Understand the media source or the outlet that you are considering pitching.

- Pitch, baby!

CHAPTER EIGHT
GAME CHANGING PRODUCTS AND SERVICES

"Sooooo now what?"

Let's say you've just shut a stage down, hopped off of the set of a local talk show, or completely turned out your latest livestream broadcast. Your audience is completely in love with you and your content, and they're convinced that you are the woman for the job. So what's the next topic of conversation between you and them?

Insert your products and services.

Your offerings are how people get to really experience you. It's one thing to hear you speak about what you do, but at some point, you have to actually *show and prove* what you do. Products and services are the demonstrations of your expertise—a tangible and real way for customers and clients to test your knowledge and for you to build your credibility (and bank account) at the same time.

Look at it like this: that late-night infomercial about that super serious pot that can make waffles, pizza, Pop-Tarts, and fried chicken (all at once) is enticing, but if you could see it in play with that nice lady in the apron at Costco, wouldn't you feel better about your purchase? Unless you just love the thrill of those late-night credit card swipes (no judgment), I'm guessing that you'd rather actually taste the food to make sure it doesn't have an aluminum flavor or actually see if it would burn up your crust *before* you spend the money.

In business, we all have to show and prove. And when you

put your knowledge into a package with a price tag on it, that's exactly what you're doing.

THE POWER OF THE PRODUCT

A business is not a business without products or services. Many people do not see themselves as product creators or service providers, but there is an opportunity for both, regardless of your industry. If you are a professional speaker, your primary service is speaking. As far as products, print books, and audiobooks are standard products for speakers. In fact, speakers, or any businesses for that matter, don't look credible without a product or service to offer.

Services are great, but the reality is a service-only business has its limitations. Until you are in the position to hire a team of clones, you can only deliver so much and serve so many people alone. Products allow you to spread your knowledge en masse without you having to be physically present. A book or a course can be created and designed once, then sold and distributed without you having to do the work over and over again.

So the reasons WHY you want to create products in your business are:

They leverage your time. The key to product creation is to develop them one time so you can focus on demand and distribution. I recently launched one of my favorite products, the Yes! Board. Now that I have designed it, all I have to do is sell, print, pack, and ship. I don't have to sit in front of my computer and create one at a time or teach a workshop over and over on the same material in order to get paid. Your books and other products are the same way. You'll find that you have more time in your business when all of your time and money is not tied up or dependent on 1:1 services.

They show people that you know what in the hell you're talking about. This goes right along with credibility. Products help you to look less janky. The fact that you have enough knowledge to put into a product speaks volumes. If you trust yourself enough to ask for money for that knowledge and to do the work involved in delivering it to someone, you send a sign to a buyer that you are an expert in your field. The entrepreneur who is always giving away something for free (or a low, low rate) and never charging for anything may as well walk around with a "Kick Me, I'm New!" sign taped to their buns. People expect experts to charge for their work and to charge what that work is worth. Low rates often signal low quality.

Umm, you're in this thing to make money, right? As a business owner, you should always, always be creating more than one revenue stream. If you offer services, great. But you need products to bring in additional flow. Never leave money that makes sense (or cents) on the table.

MAKE IT SUITE

A product suite is taking one product and building other products around it. All of those products integrate somehow, meaning they work together and support each other. Take Apple for example. If you buy an iPhone, you probably want an iPad. Once you have both of those, it only makes sense to get an iMac and why not add in an Apple TV while you're at it? And of course, you need iTunes. Congratulations—you've just been Apple-d, baby.

And it all started because you wanted to upgrade your old, raggedy cell phone. (I know. They got me too.)

I know you've been thinking that you can't show up on the set strong like Apple, but the truth is you can, and you should. All it takes is a little creativity and some thought about how you can pour what you know into a bottle and sell it.

When you create a product suite for your own business, you want products at various levels and price points, so that people can experience you in a way that best suits their needs and purses. At the same time, product suites diversify your income. If you have a few people purchasing a $20 product, a few more picking up your $700 product, as well as those who want to get in on the $10K level (absolutely they exist), you will diversify the hell out of your income. Do you see how that is more advantageous than one standard, one-size-fits-all-product?

If skinny jeans range in size, so should your paper.

Let's look at some standard options for your product suite:

A do-it-yourself, or DIY, product—This is typically your lowest tier; this may be a book or a CD series that teaches someone how to do something on their own.

A done-with-you, or DWY, product—This may be your mid-tier offering designed for you to work with the client on a limited basis, for example, in a group mastermind.

VIP—This is your premium-priced product; examples may include individual or group VIP days or 1:1 coaching programs. As a side note, I always recommend creating a "VIP" version of your regular products. You will always have clients and customers who prefer an exclusive service and who are willing to pay more for it.

I have 25 top recommended products and services that are great for bringing in the cash. Please make sure that you Activate Your Yes! at www.readyfortheyes.com to claim your free training.

Here's a sample product suite:

- 1:1 Coaching

- VIP Day

- Group VIP Day

- Book, Workbook, DVD (printed and shipped on-demand

THE ART OF PROFITS

Pricing is definitely a science, but you can earn an "A" in the class. The reality is that just like with your product suite, pricing is not a one-size-fits-all formula. What works for my business may not work for yours and vice versa. Yes, there may be some guidelines, depending on your industry, but how you decide to price your products and services is an individual choice. Still, there are some factors that you want to consider.

First, pick a pricing model that feels comfortable and aligns with your revenue goals. If your goal is to earn $100,000, you have to think about how many sales it will take to get there. You could:

- Sell 100,000 products at $1 each

- Sell 10,000 products at $10 each

- Sell 1,000 products at $100 each

- Sell 10 products at $10,000 each

Which feels like the best fit for you?

As you can see, pricing is a numbers game. The larger your fan base, the lower your prices can be because you are able to sell more products. So either you sell lower-priced products to a lot of people or you can be more exclusive and charge premium rates so you don't need thousands of clients or customers to reach your goals. For me, it's more appealing (and if I can be real, less headache) to work with fewer clients at a premium price point than to try to lay hands on a thousand people every month. I want to give my clients a top-notch experience and all of me, so I have to limit that to a small group.

When I am working with branding clients to create products and services, here are the general guidelines I use for pricing:

- VIP Days or 1:1 Coaching $1,500 (low-end) to $100,000 (high-end)

- DWY Products: $2,500+

- DIY Products: $50+

Another pricing rule of thumb is the higher the price, the longer and usually more in-depth and high-end the experience should be. On the other hand, the lower the price, the faster your customer should get what they paid for. For example, a twelve-week coaching program for $500 is out of the question.

You want people to say yes to you for the *right* reasons, and being dirt cheap isn't one of them.

YOU GET NOT BECAUSE YOU ASK NOT

Recently, I had a really sweet chick come through a Periscope broadcast that I hosted on pricing. I was discussing my philosophy on premium pricing, and she interjected with a comment that she would personally feel like a fraud for charging the price that I suggested for a premium service. *Sigh*. That hurt me to my heart to hear. But I'll say this with all of the love I can (and Momma, please cover your eyes):

If you feel like a fraud about your price, it means you don't know what the 'eff you are doing.

When you are an expert, a true, for real expert, then you should have no reservations about your rates. You should never feel like you are a fraud or stealing money from people for something that you actually know how to do. Until you can get comfortable asking for money, don't flip the switch on that "We're Open" sign. Continue to practice for free until you gain the experience and, more importantly, the confidence, to demand the fees that you deserve.

But, while some of you may legitimately need a little more experience notches on your tool belt (and that is really okay), let me go out on a limb and guess that most of you are just scared to ask for it (and that is not okay). As someone who has started at the bottom and now I'm here, I can tell you that your clients, those that really get your value and want to work with you, will pay what you ask for. Decide what you want to charge today, and that's it. Simple.

And if you're still unsure if it's right, I'll add this:

If you tell someone your rate, and their response is, "I'll think about it," you, Love, are in the right ballpark.

If no one bats an eyelash at your rates, I'd be willing to bet they are too low. Now this rule does *not* apply to your $20 audiobook or workbook (because anyone who ain't got that is just not worthy of your energy frankly), but this guideline is certainly applicable to your higher-end offerings. When you are charging $5,000 or more, that is what I like to call "Let-Me-Think-About-It Money." Your average customer is not whipping out a credit card and swiping for five grand at the consultation. You want rates that make people stop and think about the investment.

If they come back and sign on the dotted line, you know they're serious.

Products and Services Quick Start Tips:

- Decide what your annual revenue goal (or what I like to call your Big Money goal) will be.

- Choose the products and services for your product suite.

- Price each of your products according to how much money you need to bring in annually.

CHAPTER NINE
STARSTRUCK EVENTS

Events are essential for your personal brand for two reasons—you need to see and be seen. As you get more into your industry and positioning yourself as an expert, you'll naturally want to expose yourself to new information, new people, and new experiences. There are several types of events that you can check out—conferences, seminars, retreats, and online events like summits and teleconferences—that will support your professional growth and increase the number of eyeballs on you, which is never a bad thing, baby.

Let's talk about a few reasons why you want to come from behind that laptop and get out this year:

Access to what's happening right now. Regularly attending events keeps you in the know. As much as I love books, they can become outdated, unless the author decides to add more content and release an updated version. Think about it: if you are reading a book about marketing that was written and released in the 1980s, that book may have solid strategies, but it's missing a key element that you need today: social media. You can keep your finger on the pulse of what's fire in your industry by getting it straight from the sources (also known as your event hosts and speakers).

Automatic credibility. You should know by now that I will always slide credibility into any conversation around business because it's so, so important. When it comes to showing up like a pro, being seen at the hottest industry events is a must. If you pay to get into a room (especially a lot of money), others notice. You become an instant industry insider because you're in the place where few of your peers are. The information that is typically shared at the best events is exclusive, so it isn't just public stuff that anyone can find. If you're lucky enough to be there, you'll get it first.

Expansive network. One of the most frequently cited reasons to attend industry events is to network and meet new people. And while every other business coach in the world will talk to you about networking to make money and to sell somebody something, I want you to think bigger. I want you focused on the strategic connections that are available to you, which, in the long run, are worth so much more than a few sales.

Let's say, for instance, that I attend a conference and meet a woman there. We strike up a great conversation, and as it turns out, she is from the same city that my mom grew up in. (Personal connections never hurt, and neither does a little small talk.) As I listen to her talk about what she does for a living, she mentions that she is a Vice President of a major bottling company in Atlanta and she's so looking forward to retirement in a few months after climbing the corporate ladder for over forty years. I have two thoughts: One—Damn, she looks great! and Two—Nice lady, but this is not a potential client.

But, hold up!

Right before I tune out, I hear her mention that she sits on the board of an elite organization for women entrepreneurs. There are 50,000 women currently active and she'd love to have me speak at their next event.

Do you see what just happened there? Did I directly get a sale or a new client? No. But, did I leave with access to a brand new base of potential clients *and* a paid speaking gig? Hell yeah! This is why networking is not always about walking away with sales. You don't have to sell to people directly in order to get something. If you just come into the room with the right intentions, you never know what value you'll go home with.

Insight. Attending events allows you to do some first-hand research. Sometimes you have to pay for the scoop, and that's okay. At some point, you'll host your conference, workshop, or mastermind in a live setting, so you want to study how others do it. Hop on a plane or get in the car to go see how it's done. Check out the organization and flow of the event, what type of speakers were there, how each of them presented their content, and how the attendees responded to it. This will all be helpful information to you as you plan and host more events on your own.

FINDING THE RIGHT EVENT FOR YOU

As an entrepreneur, I recommend that you attend at least

four big events every year—that means at least one per quarter. You want two of those events to be industry events, but the other two should be out-of-the-box. If you are a copywriter, you may attend a beauty conference for some creative inspiration. But while you're there, you may notice some banners with some weak marketing language and introduce yourself to some salon professionals who need your writing services. Always be open to finding opportunity and creating opportunities where they don't obviously exist.

Opportunity doesn't always mean that someone wants it and asks you for it. Sometimes it means you saw it and created it.

And that's what going into fresh environments can do for you.

Think about where you can show up that may be related to your industry, but where you're unlikely to bump heads with the same people in your field. Have you noticed that you're constantly running into the same six people at every conference that you attend? It's great that everyone is supporting everyone else's events, but who's meeting new people? Who's making new connections? And who's making any money?

Speaking of coins, the price of an event says a lot about the quality of the people who will be there, both in the seats and on the stage. As you are weeding out which events to attend, use cost as one of your metrics. Free conferences tend to draw people who are cheap and are really just looking for something to do on a weekend. On the other hand, a person who pays $3,000 for an event comes with a completely different mindset. They have the business revenue or the personal income to attend a quality event, and those are the types of people you want to rub elbows and exchange business cards with. The same is true for speakers. Low-budget events will almost always feature presenters who are just starting out, so their content may reflect their level of experience. If you are coming for the content, keep your eye out for higher-priced events.

If you look closely at low-tier, low-priced events, typically the sponsors are local, small business owners, while larger, higher-priced conferences tend to be sponsored by large corporations (great sign). If you see Pepsi, Verizon, or Nike's logo on a banner, you can pretty much assume the event is top-flight. They have a brand to protect too, so chances are those companies will not publicly align themselves with a janky event. They have too much to lose.

DON'T MISS OUT ONLINE

Attending online events is just as relevant as live conferences and workshops. I've met some amazing people at online webinars, summits, and in Facebook groups. Keep your eye out for online opportunities to build genuine relationships with people. If you see something that interests you, don't just attend, but reach out to the hosts and panelists afterward to introduce yourself and share what you enjoyed or appreciated about the content. You never know where the relationship could lead.

GO BIG OR SMALL, BUT DON'T GO HOME

If you've done your fair share of research and can't find an event on or offline that does it for you, it may be a sign that you need to create your own. Take note of what's missing from the format and content from other industry events, and go for it.

Hosting your own events takes a high degree of organization, patience, and money. A smaller event could cost anywhere from $5,000 to $10,000; on the higher end, you could be looking at anywhere from $100,000 to $250,000, depending on the caliber of speakers and other factors like location.

Stepping up to do it yourself automatically shows people that you are the 'ish. It makes a statement that you know the level of responsibility it takes to put on an event, and when it's flawless (which it will be), even better. Only leaders are up to the task of producing an event, so you'll look like a boss. And when is that *ever* a bad thing?

Putting on your own show also means (and this is probably the best part) that you can do whatever you want. You don't have to be concerned with anyone else's rules—when you can start, who can speak, who to invite, what breakout sessions to have. You get one hundred percent creative control over how your event flows and rocks out. You don't have to wait for somebody—anybody—to give you your yes. You can always create your own.

Pumped? You should be! Let me give you a few planning tips:

It doesn't have to be live. I am the queen of pre-recorded content. You could very well see me kicking it at the juice spot down the street while one of my two-hour teleseminars is running on my iMac at home. I love Periscope Producer because it allows me to run previously recorded content all the time. Think about pre-recording your event and launching it live online. Virtual events also reduce your risk on costs. If no one shows up to your online summit, you would only have lost a little time as opposed to hotel, flight, and babysitter expenses (not to mention the cost to produce the event) to come across the country to an event only to be the only person there.

It doesn't have to be what everybody else is doing. You may want to do a virtual summit or virtual conference, but step out a little bit and try new formats. Executive roundtables are really cool, small events to get your feet wet. Facebook Takeovers, when companies allow influencers access to their Facebook pages to broadcast a livestream, are amazing too. Get creative.

It doesn't have to be huge. The success of your event is not always determined by the size. Start small and build your confidence. Audiences also appreciate smaller crowds, as most people are more likely to engage in a more intimate setting than in a space with 500 people. Try to keep your events to 20-40 people.

It doesn't have to be a panel. Don't be afraid of claiming the entire stage. Most people think any event has to involve 100 speakers to be legit, and that isn't true. If your content is good enough, you can easily diversify it and cover an entire day. Keeping it to just you as the keynote reduces your risk and headache. You won't have to worry about getting commitments from others and having them flake.

It can be expensive. One factor to always consider is cost. Small events can be expensive too. I've seen weekend retreats for six that cost up to $100,000 and events for 100 people where each person paid $25,000 to be there. As an event host, you will have to eat some costs, especially your first time out, so keep your people and your purse in mind. Will the people attending the event actually value what they get for the price? Ask yourself that before you make a large investment that you may not recoup.

After you've successfully hosted a few events, you may want

to jump out there and host some grand conference for tens of thousands. I love your excitement, BUT I want you to think about some things first. With great numbers comes great responsibility. The larger your audience, the more burden you'll have. You have to think about budget. Staff. Hotels and transportation. Volunteers. How many attendees are vegan? And that's not to mention your own hair, makeup, and outfits (c'mon, girl, you know we gotta look good). So take all of that into consideration. Any group over one hundred is probably too big if you are just starting out.

IF AT FIRST YOU DON'T SUCCEED...

Okay, I know what you're thinking. So let's go ahead and address the big ass pink elephant in the room.

Yes, you could fail. And, yes, you'll live.

Before you jump into planning an event, you have to define what success will look like to you. For me, success is just getting it done. If something goes horribly wrong or if I chose the wrong people to partner with, I'll have another chance to do it again, right?

Is success for you just getting it done? Is it ten people showing up out of one hundred? Is it your parents seeing you in front of a podium? Decide what success is for you, and not according to anyone else's standards. If you get there, you can't be wrong. You should see every success, no matter how big or small, as a lesson. For instance, marketing is about testing, so if no one shows up at your event, guess what? Your marketing sucks and you have to do a better job next time.

If it fails, just try again. Okay?

Event Jumpstart Steps

- Choose four events to attend this year—two within your industry and two that are unorthodox.

- Pick a date to host your first event and decide the format (online, offline, small, or big)

- Do it!

CHAPTER TEN
LET'S COLLABORATE

As tempting as it may be to run this empire alone, the truth is, you can't. You're headed for the big leagues, where the big brands play, and that means you need a squad. You need a team; people you can trust, collaborate with, and build amazing things with. Whoever said it was lonely at the top wasn't lying, but here's the thing—it doesn't have to be. Build the right team, and I guarantee you that your success will come.

Collaborations are so cool for a number of reasons:

Partnering with others gives you the opportunity to expand your audience into new territories that you may not have been able to access on your own.

You can test out new markets. If you've been considering working with doctors or mechanics, but that's not your current audience or base, you could partner with a professional peer who has already tapped into that network. You can test out your messaging or a new product without investing in a full-blown marketing campaign and gauge the response to your offerings without spending a lot of money.

You also get to learn how to establish relationships and work with others. As an entrepreneur, you can feel like you're living on a remote island, especially if you run an online business. Collaborations give you a chance to interact with people who get you and get your industry, so the two of you (or more) can build something solid.

BUT WAIT.

Before you run out there on the playground with a ball and start making new business friends, here's a word (actually four) of caution:

HAVE YOUR SHIT TOGETHER.

You don't want to put your name on anything that is remotely raggedy and neither does anyone else. Be sure your brand shows up tight online and have your stuff current and in order. When you reach out to someone about a potential collaboration, and they go to look you up and research you (as you know they will) you want them to say, "Okay, cool, that's what's up. I am interested," instead of, "Umm, you know what? I think I am booked—for the next ten years."

TWO HEADS CAN BE BETTER THAN ONE

Collaborations and partnerships are sometimes about building something together; other times, they're about getting another set of eyeballs on something that you're working on. There will be moments when you need an outside perspective. When we create anything, it becomes extremely personal to us. We can only see our projects from our vantage point and that point of view is based on our influences, beliefs, research, and knowledge. A partner can come in and see holes and flaws that you may have missed. That person may bring expertise, influence, and more strategic thought that you don't have, and that is never a bad thing.

However, when you're seeking feedback from a partner, or anyone for that matter, you want to be sure that the person is qualified to guide you. Ask for insight from people who have actually done something, and ideally something similar to what you are attempting to do. If you ever throw out the question, "So what do you think?" be sure your audience is qualified to answer. Someone who hasn't tried what you've tried or traveled in your shoes cannot give you anything worth listening to.

You always want to partner upwards and not backwards.

If there is one thing you must know before you consider a partnership with someone, it is to do your research. It's a mistake to look at someone's social media following and make a determination as to whether they'd make a good collaborator; that simply isn't enough information to make a decision. Poke around a bit and see what else you can find out. Check out websites, customer and client reviews, and content. You want as much exposure to the person as possible before you reach out.

The road runs both ways. Just as you are evaluating the credibility of your potential partners, people will be peep-ing you out too. If you spot an influencer that you'd like to collaborate with, don't assume it would be an automatic no from them just because you don't have that much clout yet. Position yourself for the yes with a plan and a tight outreach package before contacting them:

Find out more about the person. Know exactly what they do, what services they offer, and what's in their portfolio. When you do reach out, the request seems more authentic when you can speak to facts. People appreciate that you took the time to know something about them.

Have your personal brand in order, including some original content that you can provide. You want to be sure that you have some interviews that share your story, your thoughts, and give a glimpse of what you do.

Include some media clips in your request.

Offer a free product or service so the person can experience you before making a commitment.

TYPES OF TEAM-UPS

Before you hit the send button on that email to request a meeting or phone call with someone who you'd like to partner with, you should also know what you're asking for. Give some thought to the type of teamwork that makes sense for you and your objectives. Here are some to consider:

Partnerships: Partnerships tend to be long term, and demand more commitment and obligation. You may partner with someone to form a company or a joint venture like a product line.

Collaborations: Collaborations are designed for short-term efforts. It's a short stint, maybe for a single event, so you're not selling your soul to someone else. Collaborations are great for beta testing on a small scale before you jump into a full-on partnership.

Sponsorships: Sponsorships are a form of partnership between you and a company. Typically, a company gives you a large sum of money in exchange for recognition in front of your audience. You could seek sponsorship in the form of media; let's say for a television show.

Sponsorships can also be in the form of donations (clothes, electronics, product devices, product reviews, or demos). Let's say that I wanted to seek sponsorship for my livestream class. I may reach out to Blue, the company that makes the Yeti microphone, and ask for their support. I may request a few microphones to use as giveaways for my students or I could also see if they'd be willing to put together a free audio class.

Sponsorship doesn't always have to be monetary. You may need access to a building for an event or you may want to take a group of clients to Google's headquarters for a day.

Sky's the limit, so think beyond dollars to how else a company could support you in a mutually beneficial way.

Affiliates: Affiliates are about partnering with people that you would promote and trust in exchange for a commission. For instance, if you are constantly on Periscope with your iPhone, you may reach out to Apple and work out an arrangement that would pay you every time someone from your broadcast buys an iPhone. I personally make a lot of book recommendations, so it made sense for me to set up an affiliate arrangement with Amazon to get paid a commission whenever someone purchases a book that I shout out.

If I am considering becoming an affiliate for a company, here's what I think about first:

Do I trust the brand?

Have I tried the product or experienced it in some capacity?

Can I trust that if other people buy it, they'll be satisfied?

YOUR FIRST TIME

If you are thinking about your first collaboration, get clear on a few things first:

What are your goals?

What do you want out of partnering with this brand at the end of the day?

If you work with this brand, will it put you in front of people that you've never worked with before?

Do your research. Then, email the person who you are interested in collaborating with and give them a sample scenario of what a potential partnership would look like. Finally, ask for a meeting to discuss more. If that meeting goes well, it's time to move into setting up some agreements, designing marketing materials, and moving forward. Be sure to hold off on any next steps until you have an agreement in place and both parties are clear on expectations.

If you are seeking sponsorships, consider creating a sponsorship prospectus that provides all of the benefits, data (including demographics), and details about your event. Above all else, you want to show that the people in your audience or network align with the company's target audience.

For affiliates, be straightforward. You have leverage, so your outreach to the company should speak to how you use or promote the product frequently, and you'd like to find out how they are willing to compensate you if you continue to talk about it.

And remember, partnerships don't always have to be paid. You can collaborate with charities and community organizations to bring awareness to your brand. Tie your personal story into your partnerships to give people a deeper look into who you are. If you have a family member who was impacted by breast cancer, you may seek a partnership with the Susan G. Komen Foundation. If you overcame an illness as a child, perhaps Make-A-Wish is an ideal collaboration for you. There are plenty of charities out there, so explore those opportunities too.

Partnership Jumpstart Tips

- Make sure your personal brand is in order.

- Make a short list of potential partners and projects that may be a good fit for each.

- Do your research before reaching out.

- Reach out to at least one person or company to discuss opportunities.

CHAPTER ELEVEN
HIT IT OUT OF THE BALLPARK

YOUR PERSONAL BRAND QUICK LAUNCH STRATEGY

We've covered a lot in this book, right? I know your head is probably spinning! I want you to go through this book, phase by phase, step by step, and really execute each one. When you do, you'll have a personal brand that is not only powerful, but one that reaps the profit seeds that you've sown with your investments of time and money, your credibility, your expertise, and your hard work. If you do the work, you'll get the results. So don't skimp on the process.

But because I love you, I wanted to give you a fast-track version of everything we've covered in the previous chapters. I've boiled everything you need down to 15 steps. Think of this as your blueprint and checklist for launching your personal brand.

Take it and run with it!

Phase One: Personal Branding

1. Be clear on your why.

- Why are you developing a personal brand?

- Why is it important for you to do it right now?

- Take an assessment to get to know yourself (*Strengths-Finder, How to Fascinate, or Kolbe* are all great options)

2. Be clear on what you want to be known for.

- When someone thinks of you, mentions you or refers you, what should they tell people about you?

- How much experience do you have in your field? Get some experience if you feel that you don't have enough. Take classes, but also deliver the product or services. Get reviews and testimonials from the people that you work with and do it repeatedly (at least two to ten times) before you decide that this is your thing.

3. Own your name.

- Purchase your domain from GoDaddy.

- Get a branded photo shoot. Use those photos to properly promote your brand for professional speaking engagements, events, partnerships, interviews, and your own website.

- Work with a graphic designer to create your brand identity and logo. Choose your brand colors, fonts, brand patterns, and tone in which you want to deliver your content and offerings to the marketplace.

- Begin to develop your personal brand website.

- Create your social media pages and profiles and be sure they are congruent with your brand identity.

Phase Two: Speaking

4. Find somewhere to speak.

- If you have zero speaking experience, find some events where you can speak for free (and don't forget that livestreaming is a form of speaking too). If you are super scared of public speaking, try a mini phone challenge or video challenge, even if you just record yourself speaking for five days and share it with someone you trust for feedback. You could also record audios on your phone to get used to your own voice.

- Get in on an online summit or some online classes where you can be a guest expert, instructor, or facilitator.

- After you are comfortable, do as many free events as you can until you are confident that you can bring down the house.

- Start seeking paid speaking engagements. Don't rule out international opportunities or online or offline events.

Phase Three: Publishing

5. Write something and publish it to validate your ideas and perspectives. It could be a book, workbook, journal, guide, report, article, an on or offline magazine, column, blog, or vlog.

Phase Four: Media

6. Look for some media outlets that will complement your brand and serve your audience.

7. Be clear about what your desired audience is consuming. What radio shows are they listening to? What magazines are they reading? What YouTube channels are they subscribed to? How about TV shows? Television shows can tell you which networks are best suited for your audience.

8. Podcasting is a great form of media that is often over-looked.

- Try to have a mix of media in your portfolio: a TV feature, a printed publication, and a feature on a radio show or podcast.

- If you can't secure a feature of your own, having some-one mention or recommend you is just as great.

Phase Five: Products and Services

9. Identify your unique, signature way of doing something. Do you have a program or a system that you can turn into a framework? What type of signature system, framework, or ideas do you have that no one else does that you can coin as your expertise?

10. Other products that you can create or innovate include DVDs and CDs; workbooks, books, and home study programs; apparel and merchandise (like t-shirts). Services can include coaching and consulting.

Phase Six: Events

11. Make a list of events in your industry and attend one event every quarter.

12. Host some events to determine how audiences respond to your marketing, you, and your brand. Was the feedback great? Was it whack? What do you need to improve?

13. Include online events to expand your reach beyond your zip code.

Phase Seven: Partnerships

14. Determine which companies and brands are in alignment with your brand and can help you to expand and tell more people about what you do.

15. Look at some other brands who have already obtained sponsors and do some research on them. Those companies that were willing to sponsor them may be open to sponsoring, partnering, or endorsing your brand or event, or paying you a commission to promote them (affiliates).

CHAPTER TWELVE

IT'S A WRAP!

You made it!

Here we are at the end of this journey, and you are absolutely ready for the YES! I am so grateful that you have made it here. We've talked about a lot in this book, from launching your personal brand to building powerful partnerships. This process that you've just walked through is based on my signature framework, UnCloned Marketing Method. We offer various signature programs that are designed to take a deep dive into the development of your marketing systems and personal brand. Please visit **www.audriarichmond.com** to learn more about these programs.

I need you to know that you are great and beyond amazing. I wrote this book to get you ready because I know that when you are prepared, your lucrative opportunities will follow every time. I don't want you to miss out on anything that this world has for you, especially when you have everything that it takes to claim it. Whether you are holding this book in your hands or reading it on your smartphone or tablet, you have access to what other people don't--the steps to the Seven Phases framework. There's no more guessing about what to do, who to talk to, or what's next. Don't let this book catch dust and definitely don't get intimidated by what we've discussed here. You are a lot closer than you think. You can do this. There's nothing left for you to do but to GO GET YOUR YES!

Also, don't forget to Activate Your Yes! Which includes a jumpstart toolkit and additional bonuses at **www.ready-fortheyes.com.**

You can find me online on your favorite social media platform, check out the links below.

https://www.facebook.com/audriadrichmond/

https://www.instagram.com/audriarichmond/

https://twitter.com/audriarichmond

https://www.periscope.tv/audriarichmond/

https://www.youtube.com/user/audriarichmond

Until next time, let's Get You Ready for the Yes!

Love,

Audria Richmond

RICHMOND

THE YES EXPERIENCE!

When moguls like Oprah Winfrey and Steve Harvey rave about the importance of creating a vision board, they focus on turning ideas into realities. And that's where the "traditional" vision board falls short.

You see, placing pictures on a poster board to indicate your aspirations is a great way to visualize your dream life. However, if you want to live that dream life, you'll need to create and execute a strategic plan to make that dream a reality.

And that's where The Yes! Experience comes in. Created and designed by Branding and Marketing Genius Audria Richmond, The Yes! Experience arms users with the tools and guidance to transition from visionary to action taker.

No more cutting out pictures, permanently attaching them to a board and hoping for the best. The Yes! Experience, you'll get a beautiful 8.5" x 11" action-inducing vision mapping book with 100 full-color pages designed for you to take action.

In the book, you'll attach a photo of you and other images demonstrating up to 4 desires. Plus, unlike with a traditional vision board, you can identify and devise a plan to overcome what's blocking you from achieving your desires. From there, you'll record the preparation needed to meet each desire and include an "Access Granted" date once that desire becomes a reality for you.

And the best part is The Yes! Experience is a year-round activity that you can do anytime not just at the top of the year. When your desires change, you can add and remove desires as your situation changes or your mindset shifts.The

Yes! Experience also includes a companion event or course that explains how to get the best results from The Yes! Experience. Also included in this package is an "Access Granted Daily Affirmations" section that allows you to easily record your progress and celebrate your achievements every step of the way.

So if you love the vision board concept but have been desperately seeking a tool that enables you to take action on your "ask," then all you gotta do is say YES to The YES! Experience.

When you purchase your workbook you will receive this following:

8.5IN X 11IN 100 PAGES FULL-COLOR VISION MAPPING WORKBOOK: This workbook is beautifully designed to fully engage you in the process of planning for your yes. It's easy and comes with very clear instructions on what to do.

INTERACTIVE companion course: You don't have to guess what goes where. With this interactive course, we guide you step by step with video instructions so you can complete the Yes Experience with confidence.

The Yes Tribe Facebook Community: We have a community of like-minded individuals just like you who want a better life. It's your family away from home. We plan to have so much fun. Come and join the party. Learn More and Sign up at **www.theyesexperience.co**

ABOUT THE
AUTHOR

Audria Richmond is the founder of UnCloned Media, LLC, an award-winning marketing and launch consultancy for top-notch brands who want to command first-rate profits. As a highly sought-after marketing and launch strategist, Audria champions entrepreneurs to stand in front of their brands—UnCloned and unafraid to be seen. With her incomparable formula of innovation, unquenchable creativity and tech-savviness, Audria is a force that is impossible to reckon with. Audria has left her mark on personal and company brands all over the world, from the United States to Singapore and continues to do so with her elite UnCloned Marketing Membership.

She is always the woman who is thinking of—and executing on—a master plan. Since changing the game with her signature system, The *UnCloned Marketing Method*, a revolutionary system that teaches clients how to build wildly profitable marketing systems and personal brands from the ground up with the proven practices, the tools and the strategies they need to go big and stay there, she released three bestselling books in 2017, *Are You Ready for the Yes: How to Prep Your Brand for Lucrative Opportunities, UnCloned: Seven Epic (Un) Rules for Owning Your Shit,* and *The Yes Experience.*

She also lends her expertise and unconventional, never-inside-the-box perspective to her digital marketing platform the UnCloned Marketing Membership.

Meet Audria at **www.audriarichmond.com.**

Made in the USA
Columbia, SC
26 June 2021